Crash Test Parents

THIS LIFE
— WITH —
BOYS

Other books in the Crash Test Parents series:

Parenthood: Has Anyone Seen My Sanity?
The Life-Changing Madness of Tidying Up After Children
Crash Test Parents Guide to Surviving a Year*
Crash Test Parents Guide to Self-Esteem*

*Available only at www.racheltoalson.com/freebook

To see all the books Rachel has written, please click or visit the link below:
www.racheltoalson.com/store

Rachel Toalson

THIS LIFE
—WITH—
BOYS

Batlee Press
PO Box 591596
San Antonio, TX 78259

Copyright ©2017 by Rachel Toalson
All rights reserved.

No part of this book may be reproduced or transmitted in any form or by any means, electronic or mechanical, including photocopying and recording, or by any information storage and retrieval system, without permission in writing. For information, address Batlee Press, PO Box 591596, San Antonio, TX 78259.

The author appreciates your taking the time to read her work. Please consider leaving a review wherever you bought it, or telling your friends how much you enjoyed it. Both of those help spread the word, which is incredibly important for authors. Thank you for your support.
www.racheltoalson.com
www.crashtestparents.com

Manufactured in the United States of America

First Edition—2017/Cover designed by Toalson Marketing
www.toalsonmarketing.com

*To Memaw, who would have laughed until the sound shook out
Wish you were here to see this*
R.T.

Contents

Destroy: A Boy's Manifesto
3

That's Pretty Much Who They Are
35

Growing Up is Hard to Do
85

That's Just...Weird
123

The Transformative Nature of Boys
161

How to Be a Mother of Boys
211

Foreword

Boys are a force to be reckoned with. They are, by turns, danger-seeking, thrill-seeking and pleasure-seeking. They will angrily declare you the worst parent ever and promptly harvest a whole field of wildflowers so you'll know just how much they love you. They will run a lap around the cul-de-sac half an hour after they claim they're too tired to do their chore, which happens to be sweeping the floor. They are messy, distractible, impulsive, curious, and some of the most loving little people I have ever known.

When I first became the mother of a son, I had no idea that I would, at the end of it all, become the mother of six sons. I had no idea the rich and energetic life that is life with boys. My boys keep me on my toes—trying stupid things without thinking, transforming the refrigerator door into a revolving door, engaging in slap fights because it's fun entertainment.

There is never a dull moment in life with boys.

This is both blessing and curse. My boys are some of the most challenging people in my life. I often look at them in both wonder and horror. I feel an alien divide between us sometimes.

But one thing that remains consistent is that a life with boys is meant to be lived in laughter.

I hope that as you read these tales and anecdotes from the life of a woman surrounded by boys, you, too, will see the value of laughter.

Parenting is not, by any means, easy, and that's as it should be. The most transformative things in our lives are also the most challenging. Those challenges are made more joyful, more bearable, and more beautiful if laughter wins in the end.

So here's to laughter. And life with boys.

Destroy: A Boy's Manifesto

What Sons Do to a Perfectly Good House

It's amazing not only the amount of destruction my six boys can wreak on a room or a house, but *how* they actually manage it.

Everywhere I look in my house, there is a humorous story to tell. There are closet doors that don't slide anymore, because someone decided he wanted to fit between them and pretend he was a flattened piece of life-sized paper, rather than a large 3D shape. Nope. There is a ceiling fan with only three blades because one of my boys thought it could be used to swing from his top bunk to the floor. Fail. There is a piano bench that has been stripped of all its wood so that boys could whip each other's legs and see who cried first ("It's the hurting game, Mama," they said later. "That sounds like zero fun at all," I said.).

A while ago, Husband and I had to figure something out for our twins, because every time we put them down for their naps, before they would collapse into an exhausted heap of boy energy on pause, they would ransack their closet and fling all the clothes and hangers onto the floor. It took hours of our time to clean up, because they're not quite competent at anything coordinated except, of course, climbing the walls to get to those clothes.

The closet doors were the kind that slide open (the same ones our oldest broke in his own room, trying to become a pancake). So we locked the doors in place with two boards we nailed into the floor, in front of and behind the doors so our twins would not succeed in pushing the doors off their hinges. Then we took an extra precaution—we installed an actual door hinge at the top, way up high, that would prevent the doors from opening at all.

That rigged-up solution lasted all of three weeks, until our twins somehow silently pulled up the piece of wood behind the doors, even though they couldn't open them (I know. It's still a mystery to me. Also a mystery: How they could do it without noise. I sit right outside their door for the entirety of nap time.). After they demolished the booby trap, they effectively pulled the doors off the hinges and reached the treasure of their clothes again, which they spread all over the floor like a shirt carpet. So now the closet doors don't slide anymore, because we removed them and also all the clothes from closet. Six boys now share one closet, because the second upstairs closet is clearly not conducive to handsy twins. This makes whose clothes are whose a little complicated, but it's better than hanging up forty shirts every single day.

Around my house there are dying plants stripped of their prettiest leaves, torn so that boys can sword fight—or leaf fight, as I like to call it—in the middle of the kitchen. There are drawers they pull out and push back in as hard as they can to express their anger or their joy; you never know which. There is the table where they've scratched their names, the names of their family members, unintelligible words, and some personal designs, all executed with their forks at dinnertime when Husband or I turned our backs for a second because someone asked for more food. There are the nicks in all the walls where they have accidentally misjudged the distance between dry wall and their foot; the flowerpots they've broken because they thought it would be a good idea to turn a flip on the couch; the light in the kitchen they broke because one of them entreated the rest of them to play "Knights of the Roundtable" with a broom and some homemade light sabers (guess that's what I get for reading them *The Story of King Arthur and His Knights*); and the back door swaying on its hinges because to a boy, "Close the door gently," is synonymous with, "Close the door as hard as you can possibly manage, preferably so the house shakes on its foundation."

There are books that get torn in a moment of silliness, couches that sag because no one knows what "don't jump on couches" means, carpet that's caked with slobber and spit-up and mostly mud they find in the backyard like it's some kind of magnetized force. There's the bathroom tile that doesn't quite sit right anymore because taking a bath means flooding the floor with water. There are drawings all over their closet walls and their doors and the family room downstairs, because they didn't remember to keep their art on paper instead of forbidden places. There are blinds they've broken because they were too enamored with watching the trash man shake out our trash to bother with opening the slats properly. There are pieces of paper that get ripped up in a moment of "I want to see." There are crayons broken three seconds after we buy them.

There's the little kid guitar we got from a kind neighbor who knew we were musical people, which lasted all of ten days before one of the boys decided to take a scissor to all of the strings. There's the drum kit out in the garage that has been beaten nearly to death by plastic drum sticks that were never intended for a real set. There are bookshelves holding all our favorite books that look like they've also held boys. By their teeth.

Boys are hard on things. They don't pay attention to their brute strength and often don't possess the cautious care we sometimes wish they had. Husband and I have tried hard to teach our boys how to take care of their things, how to treat our home like it's important, how to still their urge to destroy things. But this is who they are.

The reality is boys are born with a joy for taking things apart—whatever that looks like—and then trying to fix them. Sometimes they find out that whatever they take apart can't be fixed. We let them learn this valuable lesson. They'll have to learn it in life, too, and toys are a smaller risk than relationships.

And though it's sometimes annoying to look around my home and see the marks of a boy here and the etches of a boy there, I also know that one day, when we repaint the walls and fix the lights and replace the couches, I will miss the stories this house has to tell.

So, for now, I choose to look around my home and embrace its destruction. Because it says surely and certainly: I am a mom of boys.

And I'm proud of it.

How Boys Destroy Everything You Thought You Knew About Bedtime

It's bedtime. A time when parents breathe a long sigh of relief and say, finally, finally, finally the job is done for the day. A time that should be rest-time for everyone—especially parents—in the whole world, if this were a perfect world.

But it's not. And just when I'm trying to tuck myself in, Husband stretched out beside me, here comes a knock on the door, and we're clocking time again.

Sometimes it's the 8-year-old coming to tell us goodnight one more time, or coming to give the baby a kiss, even though we just got the baby down for the night, or coming to say something about what he's going to do tomorrow when he gets home from school, because what he really wants to do is play with his LEGO pieces all day, and can't he stay home and do that, because it is, after all, really close to his birthday, and he really wants to do it and won't we just let him do it and don't we care about him at all, because if we did, we would let him stay home from school. I'm summarizing. This took many more words, in reality.

While this wouldn't be such an interruption with any other kid —the kind of kid you could pat on the head, say, "How about we talk about this tomorrow?" and send back on his way to bed—this kid is the one with the sticky brain, and he will fight to the death for anything and everything (because he has yet to learn how to pick his battles in order to gain an ear). This is the boy I can always guarantee will have that "But why can't" response to anything I do or say. So it'll take fifteen minutes just to get him back out of our room, especially when we tell him that we'll talk about this in the morning, because right now is not the time and we're trying to go to sleep and we're really tired and this is not an emergency. He wants an answer right now. I take that back. He doesn't want *an* answer. He wants the right answer.

Sometimes the one knocking is the 6-year-old coming back in to give us another kiss goodnight because he really missed us at school today, and then he'll tell us something cool that happened during his day, even though he already told us at dinner. He just wants to make sure we heard him when he was talking, because it was pretty riotous at the dinner table tonight, since we had asparagus to eat and everybody wanted to log their complaint (as if we haven't heard it all before). And then he'll tell us that we forgot to give him his vitamins yesterday and it's too bad that when you forget you can't have double, because he really likes vitamins, and, oh yeah, did he tells us that he tried broccoli and cauliflower at dinner tonight again and he really likes them? Well, he does, and now he wants to have broccoli and cauliflower in his lunch tomorrow, at which point Husband or I insert a "Can we please talk about it tomorrow?" and he goes merrily on his way, because he doesn't have a problem with we'll-talk-about-it-later speak.

Sometimes the door opens on the 5-year-old, who's also stealing in to give us an extra hug and kiss, after which he'll collapse on our bed and pretend he's too tired to walk *all the way* back to his room, because really he misses being with us all day. This is his first year of school, after all, and he would like nothing more than a little more time with Mama and Daddy. The problem is, we're so tired from pouring ourselves out for everyone all day that we really just want to be alone so we can sleep. So he'll ask Husband to carry him back to bed, even though Husband has already done this once before. The 5-year-old's legs are *really* tired, though, he says. Husband will roll his eyes and get back out of bed.

This ritual, in the light of day, always seems really humorous to me. The 5-year-old is too tired to walk back to bed. He doesn't even know the meaning of tired. I, on the other hand, know the meaning of tired. The meaning of tired is holding a clingy, teething baby all day and juggling two 3-year-old twins, trying to keep them out of trouble and things. The meaning of tired is managing three older boys who like to leave permanent markers where twins can reach them and mark up the whole world, including themselves. Tired is making sure school boys finish their homework and read for twenty minutes. It's signing folders and book logs and bathing everyone and doing story time and snuggling and wrestling all of them, finally, into bed. And then back into bed. And maybe, if we're really lucky, back into bed again.

This is tired. This is "I've fallen into my bed and I can't get back out" tired.

Having children has redefined what it means to go to bed. Now "go to bed" means as soon as I wrap my covers around me, that extra knock will come calling. Or the door will burst open on a boy who's scared of the dark or is having trouble sleeping, or, God forbid, needs to throw up. Or someone will cry out for me or Husband because a brother accidentally kneed him in the face.

When I first became a parent, I idealistically thought that bedtime wrote "The End" on a parent's day. But now I know that once you complete the ritual of bedtime, there are all sorts of mishaps that can come tiptoeing, tripping, and sometimes galloping through the dark. We haven't slept properly in eight years, because a parent never goes off duty.

My boys have effectively destroyed bedtime. But you know what? Science shows that a brain can think more creatively when it hasn't had quite enough sleep.

Every parent's silver lining.

How a Boy Obliterates the Remote Possibility of "Clean"

"I just wanted to show you this," the 8-year-old says one night during our family's second Silent Reading time, when the older three boys get to stay up a bit later than the younger ones and read for a few more minutes. Husband and I are usually hiding away in our room during this part of the evening, doing some reading ourselves —or, in Husband's case, falling into black holes on YouTube.

My son walks to the side of my bed, and I let him show me what he wants me to see, and I exclaim over the part in the Captain Underpants book he wants me to read, and then I tell him that's nice, thanks for sharing, now he needs to get back out where he's supposed to be and leave me in peace. I leave off that last little part, of course.

"Okay," he says, and he skips back out to the home library for the last three minutes before the timer goes off and says it's time for them to get in bed.

I don't even realize he's left the dang book on the floor until the timer clangs and I'm getting up to walk back out to the library and tell them it's time to brush their teeth and get in bed, and the corner of the book tears off my little toenail, eliciting an accidental curse from my mouth. Don't worry, Mom. No one heard but God, and I think he probably agreed.

It's the same with any room my boys enter. They have the ability to dismantle the neat and orderly look of a room in a matter of seconds. Usually no more than three. Not too long ago, we were trying to set up for a birthday party, and my mom, who often comes early so my boys aren't underfoot while I'm scurrying around, had not yet arrived. Husband asked if we wanted to set the boys up with a diversionary activity, which is code for "put on a movie," but I'm not a big TV fan, so I said no. He looked at me like I'd likely regret it, but how much trouble could the boys cause in the five or ten minutes before my mom showed up?

Turns out that answer is quite a lot.

I should know this by now. Every parent of boys knows that if you turn your back and let them roam free for any amount of time, they're going to bring a mess with them, from seemingly nowhere. It follows them around, like Pigpen from Charlie Brown. They carry invisible boxes of dirt and food and mostly popcorn kernels that they'll unleash on a newly vacuumed carpet with a single flick of the wrist.

So there I was, trying to mix together some dark chocolate icing, because I'm an annoying overachiever and make all the party food from scratch. I also, in my overachieving, like maintaining the illusion that Husband and I have some modicum of control over our home, which means it must be perfectly put together before any guests begin to arrive, so Husband was running a vacuum cleaner for the third time, because, like I said, boys and dirt. In the middle of my arranging the ham salad sandwiches on a spotless white serving tray and dumping some organic celery and carrots into another serving tray and neatly setting a tower of chocolate peanut butter whoopee pies on another tray, I heard a crash and nothing else for a minute, until Husband said, "No, no, no, don't get that out, we're setting up for a party and we want to keep it nice and neat in here."

It's a good thing he was the one to address them, because I likely would have been screaming. Not really. But maybe.

I knew that I probably didn't want to see what all the commotion was about, but I'm also the sort of person who likes to know what's going on at all times, so, against my better judgement, I peeked around the corner of the kitchen, and it was astounding what kids did in the living room in less than a minute. Less than sixty seconds. I guess that's a relatively long time the life of a child. Because somehow the 5-year-old had already grabbed a stack of coloring books and crayons and dumped them all out on the table we'd use to seat people for the lunch we were planning to serve. The 6-year-old had rummaged through the game cabinet and found Battleship so he could have it ready to play with his grandmother when she got there, except the rummaging unleashed what tenuous hold that game cabinet had on organization, and there was an avalanche of game pieces that spilled out from their hiding places. The 3-year-olds had miraculously slipped past all of us and climbed up the stairs to throw down 10,000 stuffed animals that were mostly in a pile but one that was stuffed behind a couch. The 8-year-old had taken down a whole basket of LEGO pieces because he really wanted to compare all the ones he already had with the ones that he was probably going to get at his birthday party today. The baby was sitting happily in his seat, but he's the only perfect one.

It felt like all our work had just been completely undone.

This is the way it is with kids. We'll clean up a house so it's perfectly in order for one minute, and then they'll decide they want to run around in their underwear, and before we know it, we've got some clothes laid out in various crime scenes on the floor. They know better than this. They know where every laundry hamper is in the house, and there are many. But can they be bothered to put their clothes away? Nope.

We'll mop up a spill courtesy of the largest glass of milk you've ever seen, which someone tried to pour for himself and misjudged not only the volume of the cup but where the cup was positioned on the floor and then, in his horror at the mess unfolding before him, he dropped the open jug of milk, and once the floor is spotless again, we'll pour the poor boy another glass of milk, and he'll drop it on his way to the table.

We'll organize all the books back on their bookshelves, smile to ourselves and congratulate our good efforts, and then we'll turn our backs for a minute and turn back around to see that someone has tried to pull one book down and the whole shelf fell instead, and now there are ninety-two books scattered across the floor, and they don't know how to fix the hanging-by-a-screw shelf.

Boys will walk into a room and forget they've brought anything with them until you stub a toe, or, worse, puncture the heel of your foot with it (dang you, LEGO Ninjago swords). They will dump out a bin of tiny toys and clean them all up except the one your knee will find when you kneel down to check underneath the couches. You will steam clean your floors so you can finally stop looking at all those boiled egg yolks smashed into the tiles, and they'll minutes later track in a whole pound of mud from the mud pit they've been digging out back to expose the earth's core.

They'll pull out their school papers and toss them on a counter we just cleaned off. They'll stick their shoes in a basket until they're piled up with ten pairs they don't need, and the ones they actually do need were left out back, underneath the trampoline. They'll play with the trains and then decide to put on a puppet show, and they won't even know what they're doing, because the mess doesn't register in the brain of a boy. They know how to make them, but they don't know how to define them.

"It's so messy in here," I'll say, to which they'll reply, "Where?"

I've come to learn in my years with boys that sometimes I just have to be okay with mess. I just have to let that mess in, because otherwise I don't know what else to do with it, and I will go crazy trying to keep up with everything. Because every time I wipe down a counter, someone finds a tube of toothpaste and tries to aim it at a toothbrush and completely misses, and then, because it's there on the counter now, he'll paint pictures with the stickiness, because why not?

So I just do what I can. I limit where I must. And then I leave the rest to the entropy of boys.

One of these days, I tell myself, my boys will know what it means to be clean.

This is How a Parent Benefits from Boy Destruction

We shouldn't have even wasted the money.

We knew better. I mean, we've had eight years to know better. But when we were outside in our cul-de-sac, playing with our boys, and a neighbor mentioned he was going to be selling his house, and we instinctively looked up at our house to appreciate it and remind ourselves that we love it, those blinds.

THOSE BLINDS.

When our homebuilders built our house, they had the brilliant idea to put the children's rooms—or guest rooms for a couple—facing the street. If I were a homebuilder, do you know where I would put the extra rooms? Way in the back. I might not even put a window.

The blinds that line our boys' windows have needed replacing for quite some time. They were broken in stages. One line fell apart when a foot accidentally hit it while boys were wrestling in their beds. One surrendered when it saw a hand coming to peel it back from the window so a boy could look out at the trash man one fine Monday morning. The rest of them wilted when twins moved into the room, deciding all at once to give up the fight to cover a window properly.

So we replaced them, and everything looked beautiful from the street.

For about three days.

That's all it took for our twins to realize there was something unbroken in their room and decide that they must BREAK IT.

They didn't just break the brand new blinds, either. They massacred them. The blinds are dead. You can't even really tell they used to be blinds.

We don't know exactly what happened. Our twins are like ninjas. They're crafty and opportunistic and smart. That's always been the problem. One will distract the parent on duty while the other destroys something. Somehow, without our noticing, they ripped every one of those individual rows of blinds completely in two.

How? Your guess is as good as mine. The only thing I can admire about it all is that it took some determination to rip them all in two. They're faux blinds, which means they bend before they break. Our twins must have bent them thousands of times before the blinds ever broke. And they did it all silently, without our ever even guessing what they were up to.

It shouldn't have surprised us, either. These are the same two kids who single-handedly tore apart their cribs when they were sixteen months old. And by tore apart, I mean *destroyed*. They weren't cheap cribs either. They were $400 cribs, to be exact, made from sustainably harvested wood. We salvaged one of them for the baby, but the other was beyond repair.

They're the same two kids who somehow wriggled out of footie pajamas zipped up backwards (the feet were cut off) and zip-tied at the top so there was only enough room to breathe (this having been done because they went through a month-long jaunt wherein they emptied their bowels, took off their diapers, and fancied themselves wall and crib artists). They're the same two kids who overturned a heavy table bolted to the wall, doing God knows what.

All that aside, destruction in a house of all boys shouldn't come as a surprise at all. It's not just our twins. It's boys in general. Boys who think that hanging up curtains equals an invitation to try to pull them down and that installing a ceiling fan is an invitation to try it out as a carnival ride and that a distressed piano bench is an invitation to strip more wood from the seat and play with the "wood whips" while chasing each other around the house.

Boys and destruction are the best of friends.

Boys have minds that think taking the screen off an upper floor window and stepping outside on the roof is a *good idea.* They believe that playing a game on scooters where one person is "it" and the rest try to run over his toes is a fun game. They think a pair of scissors sitting next to a perfectly fine tie means they should cut it up into little pieces, because someone obviously wanted them to do this, right? Why else would the scissors be sitting beside the tie?

Because of the boys who live inside my home, I now have a dirty wall that extends from the bottom of my stairs to the top, because they like to trail their hands anywhere but the stair rail that actually serves this purpose. I have poetry books with no jackets. I have a piano bench that pinches your cheeks when you sit on it. I have fans with only four blades and butter knives that are bent in two from trying to dig to the mantle in our backyard and I have two dressers with no more working drawers. I have 4T shirts with holes in their center because someone wanted to see what would happen if they used scissors on it. I have bed frames that have given up their squeaking because they're tired and now rest on the floor instead of perching above it. I have a kitchen table with more etches on it than a 100-year-old's face.

This is life with boys.

It's maddening trying to keep up with what they'll unleash their havoc on next. But I also pretty much love it.

Because there is something else they destroy, too.

Me.

And not just because everything in my house bears the mark of their hands but because *I* bear their marks.

They are taking me apart with their destructive little hands, and this is exasperating. But it is also beautiful.

Because, you see, who I used to be before? That person concerned with how my house was put together just so, how I didn't want people to walk in the door and think, "Wow, kids definitely live here," that woman who tried obsessively to protect all the "stuff" instead of living? She was much less interesting and likable and kind than who I am now (and, consequently, more judgmental).

I am not who I once was. This is the beauty of boy destruction.

Now excuse me while I go tackle the 3-year-old who's ripping paper into tiny little confetti pieces. I think the paper might be something important.

The Mysterious Destruction that No One Claims

Set my boys loose in a room, and it's only a matter of time before everything in it falls apart.

It's not that boys do this on purpose. It's just that it inevitably happens. They'll be standing, innocently, in the middle of a room, and a fan blade will fall off. If they get anywhere close to the boxed fan, it combusts without their even laying a hand on it. If they look at their beds, the middles will start to sag in defeat. If they think about their stuffed animals, seams begin to rip apart.

This destruction follows my boys around the house daily. I watch it happen in the kitchen, where they take out bowls and spoons and then sneak out to the backyard and try to dig to the earth's mantle because someone (probably Husband) told them it could be done. The spoon, of course, comes back in all bent and misshapen so we won't be able to eat with it, but no one actually touched it, they say. They were just *pretending* they were going to dig to the mantle. They actually used their hands.

I watch it happen when they move closer to the paintings they perfected last week, putting their grubby little hands all over them so smears of dirt join the smears of yellow and red in a perfectly shaped fingerprint for which no one in the house is actually responsible. Maybe it was a robber, they say. Coming in to steal a valuable painting. I'm sure that's it, I say.

I watch it happen to the blinds, which will either snap upon notice or, if we're having a really fun day, will attract Sharpie marker prints that look suspiciously like the 3-year-olds had a grand old time when Mama was putting the laundry in the dryer. They have no idea who did it. Not even the one with black lines all over his chin.

Probably the most notable thing inside the house that no one destroys is their bedrooms. Somehow, according to them, they didn't put all those clothes on the floor, it just happened. They have no idea how it happened and now they're wondering how it is they're going to get it all cleaned up before technology time. I could care less, honestly, because I'd rather they were reading instead of watching a screen. They also definitely did not shove all their stuffed animals off their bed in a tumble of bears and dogs and big-eyed lions.

Other things they didn't touch are the colored pencils fanned out on the floor, the art notebooks stacked on the dining room table, the jump rope draped across the couch, the clothes they wore to school today, the backpacks that are still in the living room instead of on their hooks, the LEGO pieces that have exploded all over the floor. And they most definitely don't know who took their bed apart, because they specifically remember making it up this morning.

We must live with a ghost who likes pranks.

It's not just the indoors, either. Something also destroys our yard. Not only is that where bikes and roller blades and scooters get left, even though no one touched them, it's also where things like forks and spoons and the bowls that held their snack end up, even though they didn't bring any of that outside.

Step into our yard, and you will find all manner of things. Jackets, hats, scarves (because you don't need any of these for a Texas winter anymore), shoes, and, my favorite: holes. Since my oldest learned all about the earth's core, he has made it a goal to dig all the way down. And their hole is getting there, because last time I fell in it someone had to throw a rope down to pull me back out.

They accidentally cracked the tiles we used to build a fire pit. They didn't mean to tear holes big enough to swallow my backside in the wicker patio chairs. They thought when I said, "Don't pull up all the rocks around the rose bed" I meant, "Please collect all the rocks around the rose bed and make sure you fling them into our brand new air conditioning unit."

But all of this is nothing compared to the things they bring indoors with them, which causes the destruction of a mama's sanity. There are the tree limbs that they'll place neatly on my bed, because they want me to make them into magic wands. There are the jars of roly polies they arrange on a pantry shelf so I think I'm getting out a jar of sunflower seeds when it's really a bug graveyard. There are the spiders they'll bring in with them and drop, delightedly, in my lap with a quick, "Look what I found!"

The destruction boys cause is quite baffling, sometimes. They look at a brand new sock, and the sock grows a hole. They eye a bunch of bananas, and the bananas are magically gone. They find a hidden plunger and, well, you don't want to know.

But what I'm always left with at the end of a destructive day is this: memories.

The hole in the wall over there happened when somebody accidentally slammed the door too hard, which made a picture fall, which made a boy try to catch it and, instead, drive his hand through the wall. The nick on the edge of this bookshelf happened because a boy got a little too excited about a new book he'd gotten, and, in his turning around to show his brothers, he forgot that he was dressed up as Leonardo the Ninja Turtle, and his sword crashed into wood. The paleolithic cave drawings on the back of our house happened because someone let a ghost borrow a magic marker.

Boys are careless, curious, and experimental. It's just who they are.

Although, if you were to ask them, they would have a point of clarification: It's not them doing the destruction. It's someone else. We must have some kind of monster living here. Or maybe we have a ghost. I bet our house is built on a burial ground.

All I know is whichever ghost is responsible for the destruction that comes from a plunger, a used toilet, and bathroom walls is about to be sent into the beyond.

A Candid Look at What It's Like Living With a Human Tornado

Maybe it's because I'm the mother of boys, but I am telling you what. Every day, when I come down from holing up in my room and writing a handful of essays and some fiction stories, it looks like six tornadoes have ripped through the house. Make that an F6 tornado.

One shoe is sole-up by the front door, and the other is halfway across the house, in the kitchen trash can, because someone thought it would be funny to kick off his shoes as soon as he walked in the door from playing four-square outside. Sure, he saw his left shoe hit the trash can and slam dunk, but he wanted to show his daddy, who wasn't around at that very moment, and then he forgot all about it, until someone dumped a diaper that hadn't been properly closed but had been, alas, properly filled right on top of it. Now it's a speckled brown shoe that needs to be washed, pronto.

A banana peel is face down on the floor, right inside the back door so that when someone, who shall remain nameless, walks inside, her shoe will catch on it and she'll go sliding like she's a cartoon character, all the way to the counter on the opposite end of the kitchen. I think I pulled a muscle trying to avoid doing the splits. There's also a neat little stack of orange peels mashed into the cushion of the couch, where no one is allowed to eat, and over there by the kid-tent that sits in our living room is what looks like a handful of almonds that was dropped in a trail along the carpet. At least I hope it's almonds. I don't really want to know if it isn't.

All around my house, you'll see the pitiful sight of dying plants. This is not because I have a black thumb. On the contrary, if I didn't have kids to feed every day, I probably still wouldn't remember to water the plants. But that's not the point. It's really the fault of my children that all my plants have given up. You can tell who's to blame by the shape of their leaves, which are Jagged Oval, or, if you want better specifics, Handprint Oval. It's as if a kid slammed his hand against a leaf, and that portion of green, rather than hold its ground, tore out of the way. Which was probably wise, if you ask me. I've felt the force of one of those hands—accidental, of course—when I walked into a slap-fight, which is my boys' idea of a fun game. My thigh is still sporting the handprint.

Only split seconds after I summon the effort to make my bed, which isn't often, and then disappear downstairs to prepare breakfast, one of the twisters will come into my room and sneak beneath my covers, throwing all my pillows off my bed. So when I come back upstairs to wake them all, I'll see my bed and do a double take. Didn't I make it up? I guess it was just my imagination. And as I'm standing there analyzing, trying to figure out if I'm crazy or not because I can't remember whether I actually made up my bed, the twister will leap out from under the covers and scare me so efficiently I have to change my pants. Which isn't saying much, actually. That bladder control takes a hit every kid you carry.

Every Monday, I do the laundry and separate it into neat little piles so boys can put their clothes away, and within a few minutes, they will decide they'd like to flip over the side of the couch, which is piled with laundry, remember, and all my work? That's right.

Undone. After which I turn away, pretend I haven't seen anything, and let their daddy deal with the mess of one pair of underwear hanging from the art cabinet, a lone sock dusting the top of the piano (thanks, lone sock) and another pair of skivvies on the 5-year-old's head.

Most of the time my house looks like a paper explosion happened in slow motion, because six tornadoes and art don't equal neat. Papers line our floor and the love seat no one wants to sit on (because it draws its lovers to the middle) and the top of our dining room table, which is, honestly, a better option than glass (what were we thinking ten years ago? Oh, that's right. "We don't have kids!"). Papers become towers, which become carpets, which become bins and bins of recycling. It's the same cycle every week. You'd think we would set up a system. But we're too lazy for something that complicated.

My twisters destroy the home library (books are all over the floor), mutilate the kitchen when they try to get their own snack (the most recent mutilation: raw oats sprinkled on the floor, along with some drops of milk to create a nice sludge), and disfigure their room with one night of "I think I'll clean up," which, to them, means taking all the art out of their art folders and "reorganizing" it. Somehow, the papers never make it back where they're supposed to go.

And then there's what they do to a parent's room. My kids are not supposed to come into my room. But they always do. They like to leave little love notes in my bed—like sticks they find outside or the remains of a flower they picked with way too many roots still attached, including the dirt that goes with it, or the bath toys they're hiding from their brother, which are still so wet that when I get into bed, someone will have to pull me out of the puddle.

They take things out of my drawers—like the highlighter they left in the hallway instead of replacing it where it belonged, which means their 4-year-old brothers will pull off the cap and write all over the walls in fluorescent pink, saving me the trouble of actually painting the walls the color I always wanted them to be. They drop treasures into the hole in Husband's guitar so the next time he picks it up he'll be able to not only strum strings but also shake a maraca. They walk right out of their clothes and pretend they don't even notice. Or maybe they're not pretending.

Well, I notice.

But you know what? It's not so bad living with six tornadoes—because at least the next time a tornado comes through this area, I'll be prepared for the cleanup.

After all, I've practiced every day.*

*This essay published on Babble and is the property of Disney but was reprinted with permission in this book.

The Many Items of Clothing Boys Effectively Destroy

I mentioned to some friends the other day that I needed to break out the hand-me-downs for my baby. They looked at me like I was a little crazy and said, "Wait. You have hand-me-downs, after five kids?"

I laughed, because I know what they're thinking. My answer is that Husband and I didn't dress our babies very often but usually let them lie around in a onesie or maybe just a diaper and skin. Once we had our twins, we sort of gave up. They spent the first three years of their lives running around in diapers and underwear.

But now it's become more imperative that our twins wear clothes, because they're 3 and we have finally fought our way to the surface of parenting, so we're getting out more. The problem is that finding clothes for my 3-year-olds has become quite challenging, to say the least. Mostly because everything I pull out of the closet has at least one gaping hole in it.

I don't know if this is because my twins are really hard on clothes or whether it's because all those clothes have first gone through three other boys before they even got to my destructive Dennis the Menaces, but I do know that by the time the baby gets to size 3T, he will have to walk around mostly naked, because there will be nothing left. There are holes in socks, holes in jeans, holes in shirts, holes in underwear (which Husband recently told me shouldn't actually be passed down, but whatever), holes in every possible thing you can imagine.

Holes in socks are understandable. They're a normal part of life. Even though I've had socks that have lasted for fifteen years, Husband has to replace his every two years. There is no logical explanation for this except that Husband's socks not only attract holes, but they also attract starch. And by starch, I mean the sort of stiffness where when socks come out of the wash, they look as though someone pinned them to a cork board. They're perfectly straight, but if you try to bend them, they crackle.

I've given up on matching socks right out of the wash, obviously, and it's never hard to tell which ones are mine, because not only are mine silky soft but they're also bright pink and bight purple, because when you live in a house full of males, you have to do something to set yourself apart. I choose purple socks.

It's always astounding to me, however, how many of the socks I stare at in a messy pile on my bed and refuse to fold into pairs are missing their mates or riddled with holes. Some of the socks I bought two weeks ago already have holes. It's like they're walking around on a bed of cacti—which, to be fair, is pretty much any yard in Texas between the months of March and October. No grass grows here anymore. It's given up in the heat.

I know my boys walk outside in their socks, and the hay out back likes to stick to them and pull the fibers apart. I also know that sometimes they'll wear their socks on their hands so they can have a decent slap fight, and a renegade finger will find its way through a weakening section (usually the toes). I know that sometimes they strip them off when they're done playing "Slippy Slide" on the trampoline and leave them out for the wild animals that inhabit our yard—a black squirrel in particular—every evening.

So it's no wonder that there are holes. The only time we're really concerned is when one of them comes home and tells us that tomorrow at school he gets to take off his shoes during class. This will necessitate a quick trip to the store for some new socks that will be holey in less than forty-eight hours.

The holes my boys forge in jeans are also understandable, when you look at it from a child's standpoint. What is more fun than sliding across the ground on your knees? What is more comfortable than walking across a floor on your knees? What is more effective than playing chase across a blacktop on your knees?

If I tried any of these things, I would not be able to walk for months, but therein lies the joy of childhood.

My boys can often be seen scooting along cement sidewalks without wincing. They can be seen wrestling Husband (who will be sore for days and will also rip a few holes in his jeans—though those holes are not in the knees but somewhere else that render jeans entirely unwearable), bouncing toward him like a bunny rabbit—that's right, on their knees. They can be seen dragging one another by the hands across the back yard, because they're playing a "Dead Body" game, while the hay tears their jeans apart.

When I think about the jeans and all those knee-holes, I can almost feel glad that I live in Texas, where winter only gets down to about 70 degrees, which means my boys likely won't even need the jeans they've just torn up. In fact, most of the time, they wear gym shorts or sweat pants. Why bother spending money on jeans with knees blown out when I can spend money on sweatpants with knees blown out, or, better yet, shorts that don't need knees?

Holes in shoes are a bit more mysterious. We budget to purchase school-approved shoes twice a year, because it only takes a month for a boy to ruin new shoes. We stretch this ruining into four months, and by the time we're ready to replace tennis shoes, their soles are flapping and their sides are splitting. I have no idea how this happens.

Two days after buying the 6-year-old a new pair of shoes, the color on the toes was already worn off. "What are you doing to your shoes?" I said.

"Nothing," he said. "I just walk in them."

I watched him walk, and it's true, he was just walking. I watched him run, and he was just running. I watched him ride his scooter and try to stop himself from hitting a fence post, and that's when I solved the mystery. He used his toes like brakes. Step with the left foot, brake with the right, step with the right foot, brake with the left. It slowed him down and he missed the post, but, alas, his shoes were not spared.

I imagine that on their school playground, they're probably kicking things and climbing things and crawling across things, all of which take a toll on that expensive footwear. I've tried to figure out a way where I can just have them go everywhere barefoot, but then I'd have to clip their toenails. No thanks.

Holes in shirts happen mostly accidentally—say, when someone leaves out a pair of safety scissors and someone else, who is completely incompetent and should not be allowed to use scissors, discovers them momentarily and goes to work on his shirt. One of my boys cut out two perfect holes in one of his shirts so that his nipples could peer through. It was completely accidental, because he was only 3 at the time and could hardly coordinate his fingers, but was it accidental? We still don't know the answer to this question. The 3-year-old, when we asked, said, "I askidentally used the scissors." Well, that clears things up.

Holes also happen in shirts when my boys are running through the wilderness, which we try to allow as often as we can, since their balls of energy far exceed our own in strength and stamina. They run without even thinking, and sometimes a tree snags them for a moment—but only a moment, until they rip free and their shirt pieces flutter to the ground.

The holes in underwear, well, that's probably too personal. Suffice it to say that my boys come with a whole lot of gas, and sometimes that gas can blow holes in Captain America's face.

There aren't many pieces of clothing that escape the destruction of boys, and that's just talking about one specific destruction: holes. There's also markers (permanent ones, preferably), food and table manners, snot, and neglect.

In short, boys are really good at destroying clothes in a whole lot of ways, some more disgusting than others.

So I guess I should count myself lucky that I have any clothes at all to pass along the line. Even if it is the camo no one wanted.

That's Pretty Much Who They Are

When a Boy Wants to Run Away and a Mom Wants to Let Him

If I make it through a day without hearing the words, "I'm just going to run away," I wonder what went wrong.

My boys say these words to me when I tell them that their chore this week is not doing the dishes, it's sweeping the floor. Everybody, of course, hates to sweep the floor—including, and probably most of all, me, which is why I make my boys do it. The problem is that all their friends don't have parents who make them do chores (according to my sons). The problem is also that they want to go out and play with those friends who don't have parents who make them do chores, and sweeping the floor is keeping them inside for an unnecessarily long time.

They say these words when we tell them that it's time to take a bath. We only bathe them every other day because it's better for their skin and mostly we don't want to fight through bath time every single night, so we only hear this in relation to bath time every other night. They say this because they don't want to get in the bath while everybody they know gets to play outside until it's past dark, and, besides, they like smelling like a locker room.

They say these words when we announce so cheerfully that it's time to go to bed, and they want to stay up reading a little while longer, even though they weren't really reading, they were wrestling each other on the recliner in the library while someone called out literary phrases that made it sound like they were reading. They also positioned a few books in a spread on the floor beside them so they could quickly grab them when Husband and I walked into the room to see what they were doing, as if we couldn't hear the recliner's groans and their own giggles as they held each other down for the count. Also unfortunately for them, their reflexes have not quite caught up with their brains, so the books they'd put beside them did not actually make it into their hands before Husband and I charged into the room.

They tell me they want to run away when they find out what's for dinner and they haven't even tasted it. They tell me they want to run away when I let them know it's time to clean up the LEGO Explosion (it's a proper name in our house) that happened in our dining room so we can eat now, and, more importantly, walk without slicing our soles open. They tell me they want to run away when I wake them up in the morning and announce cheerily that it's time to get ready for school, and they would rather go someplace that's never heard of school.

They never have a plan, of course. I'm not really sure if they even have a destination in mind, and occasionally Husband and I will ask them. They always give a vague answer, something like, "To my friend's house," to which we will reply, "And you think that will be better than here," to which they will reply, "Well, it doesn't have to try hard," to which we will reply nothing and only capture it in our memory to write down for another time and place where it's safe to laugh.

They don't *really* want to run away. They've occasionally tried, but they didn't try very hard. Our older boys are given freedom to play in the cul-de-sac out front, so they'll slam out the front door, throwing those words back, and then, in a few minutes, when they realize they don't have a plan, they'll come walking back in. Sometimes they just need the space to be angry. I don't mind this. In fact, I remember planning to run away when I was a kid. One time I actually did, when my mother refused to take me to twirling practice. I was 12 years old and walked three miles down the road before she came to pick me up in the car. I had my baton and little else. I'm not sure what I thought I would do with a baton and little else, I just know that I assumed she would pick me up—which she did. I also assumed that she would then take me to the twirling practice in question, because I'd shown her I wasn't afraid to run away. She turned around and drove me back home, and I fumed.

So I don't get offended by my boys' declarations. In fact, sometimes I let them run away with those declarations. They wish for a family that doesn't make their kids do chores. They wish for a family that never takes baths and lets their kids stay up as long as they want every night. They wish for a family that cooks better dinners and lets them eat with a LEGO-piece carpet under their feet and keeps them home from school. I don't think such a family exists, so I let them wish.

But sometimes, when they say they want to run away and I've just spent the last thirty minutes of my time fighting with them about how they're not going to watch a movie right now, they never get to watch a movie on school nights, sometimes I want to throw my hands up and say, "Go ahead, then. Do it. I'll see you later."

It used to bother me a whole lot when they said they wanted to run away, because, as a mom, I immediately went to the place where they don't appreciate all I do for them, where they don't love me the way I should be loved, where they are selfish and ridiculous and need to learn gratefulness. But I know that running away is not about me at all. It's not about our home, it's not about our family. It is, really, only about anger. And anger is a necessary emotion. Running away, or the threat of doing it, is a byproduct of that anger —a byproduct that is relatively harmless compared to the other potential byproducts (as long as they don't actually run away, of course). So over the years, rather than feeling offended that they want to run away from this house, I feel mostly grateful that they're sharing their anger and disappointment with me. Anger and disappointment are good for children, because it means they have not gotten what they want. And not getting what they want teaches them how to accept when something cannot be changed and how to move on from the disappointment, how to fail and try again, how to be a human being. We all know adults who have never learned these lessons, and they're certainly not my favorite people to be around.

I know my boys, at least now, while they're young, will not actually follow through with their threat, because they'll get two blocks down the road and realize they forgot their shoes. Or they'll get four blocks down the road and realize they're hungry and they have nothing to eat, and how are they going to survive without food every half hour? Or they'll get all the way down to their elementary school's entrance, which is only four blocks away for those who are concerned, and they'll realize that they haven't fully thought this through, because where are they going to go and who are they going to go with, and, gosh, all these books they brought with them (because my boys wouldn't be able to leave without a thousand books stuffed inside their backpacks) are really heavy, and they're never going to make it. So they'll turn around and come back home.

In the end, they know where love lives, and it is here in this home, here in my eyes and arms and heart.

The Way to a Boy's Heart is Through His Stomach

Before Husband and I got married, I made a cake for his twenty-first birthday and toted it out to a park in San Marcos, Texas, home of Texas State University, where I had graduated college the day before. I painstakingly arranged all those Reese's Pieces around the iced-chocolate sides. It was a two-layer cake, so it was large and impressive. I watched the delight on his face as he cut into it and it promptly fell apart.

I gasped in horror. Husband laughed. It was still cake, he said, and he loved cake.

I knew then, young as I was, that food was the way to a man's heart.

Now I have six boys to feed, along with their daddy. So I know that there was never a truer adage than the one that says, "the way to a man's heart is through his stomach," because every other minute my boys open the refrigerator and search for something good to eat, particularly when Husband or I are not paying the least bit of attention. Six pounds of grapes can be gone in less than ten minutes, in case you were wondering.

The problem with this adage, however, is that I'm not really all that great a cook. I can plan like the best of them, and I can gather all the ingredients and have a recipe sitting in front of me, but when it comes to actually putting all those ingredients together and, especially, cutting up raw chicken, I lose my steam and motivation.

There's something about chopping vegetables and browning meat that feels exhausting to me.

It might be because the moment I start cooking dinner, the baby starts crying because someone accidentally poked his eyeball with a finger. And then the 3-year-old twins start secretly taking out all the art supplies they're never allowed to get down on their own, and I don't see it because I'm slaving over a burner on the stove—and they know this, and they'll milk their independence for all it's worth. Typically, around this time, the 5-year-old will find a permanent marker and draw on the back of the house, and the 6-year-old will dig in the dress-up basket to find this one particular Spider-Man glove that he just has to have, and the area around the dress-up basket will look like a groundhog has burrowed down to the wicker. Also around this time, the 9-year-old will decide, because there are no eyes fastened on him, to dump out three whole bins of LEGO pieces, which are my favorite.

Generally speaking, my boys are supposed to have mandatory play-outside time while their Daddy or I are cooking dinner, but when I'm trying to make sure I'm not scalding the almond milk that is thickening in a pot for a bit of gravy, while trying to keep the sputtering pan of chicken from making too big a mess, I'm not really all that concerned with why the back door keeps opening and closing and how many kids have passed through it to remain inside, because they see that my attention is effectively divided. I've even attempted to lock the 3-year-old twins out back, because while my older boys have the privilege of playing out front with all their friends, the 3-year-olds can't be trusted with anything so sophisticated as freedom in a cul-de-sac, but somehow, some way, my twins have learned how to pick the lock, and, besides, Husband sometimes forgets to lock his shed, where they've found such treasures as an adult-sized shovel they used to sword fight before someone nearly had their head knocked off, some car wash supplies they poured out all over the backyard, and a gas tank full of gas they dumped into a hole they're digging to the earth's mantle.

No thanks.

So while I once enjoyed the cooking part of "food is the way to a man's heart," I no longer enjoy it nearly as much.

However, when I actually do suck it up and find some energy from somewhere in the amazing storehouse moms have despite the energy toll of their children, and I actually get something that looks remotely appetizing on the table so that boys are tempted to try it, they will, after dinner, bombard me with hugs and thanks and say it's the best dinner ever (except, of course, the one who complains about everything we have for dinner without even tasting it first).

When I've cooked treats for them, which isn't often, because sugar and boys make me shudder, they are so excited they nearly knock me over with their gratitude. On their birthday parties, when I go all out with both food and sweets (though not Pinterest-worthy, we must establish that right now), they hug me fifty times during the course of the party, saying I'm the best mother ever. This, of course, is good for the self esteem, considering that this morning, before the birthday party, they told me they wanted to run away because I wouldn't let them dump out the LEGO pieces, since we were about to have a house full of 6-year-olds.

The same is true for the days we've taken them out to pizza buffet, because that's the only pizza you can afford when you're the parent of six boys. They love pizza buffet. They love food. We're the Best Parents Ever.

Conversely, the times that we have told them they've had enough to eat—usually because they've inhaled two pounds of bananas in as many minutes—they call us the Worst Parents Ever. Using my mathematical logic, which I honed in Mrs. Allen's algebra and calculus classes, this tells me that food equals love to boys.

So, every now and then, I surprise them with pizza or chocolate chip cookies or an ice cream party where our family is the only one invited. These surprises are the times when I can see their love tanks filling before my eyes. I'm a mom. Of course I want to feed my children well, and I do it pretty obsessively most days of the week. But there are also times when I let loose the reins and we have ourselves a stomach-turning chips and salsa marathon.

Fill their bellies and hug them a lot. It's really not that hard to raise a boy.

Well, actually, it's a lot harder than that. But this is what I'll tell myself today, as I'm slaving over some broiled chicken parmigiana with roasted asparagus, which I know is going to elicit some all-too-familiar complaints.

A mom's gotta have some kind of motivation to ignore the circus happening in her living room while dinner's browning.

The Messy Child: He's Likely Not Going to Change

Every parent needs that one child who makes a mess wherever he goes.

I know what you're thinking. Isn't that most children? Yeah, probably. But some of them are trainable. This perpetually messy child? Not so much.

I've tried training this kid of mine for nine whole years of my life, and I still have to say the same things over and over and over again. Put your bowl away when you're finished eating your oatmeal. Put your shoes where they go so you can find them easily tomorrow. Please don't leave that book in my room, because it's yours and I'm not going to read Pokémon right now. My book list is way too long already.

Sometimes I can get pretty fed up with telling him the same things over and over and over again. What is so maddening is that sometimes he will surprise me and do something completely outside of his normal mode of operation—like shut the refrigerator door when he's done digging for food without asking. And other times he forgets his shoes when he walks out the door.

I know that part of the problem is that he exists in a highly creative world that's all his own. He is always thinking about the movies he's going to make when he gets older—or the stop motion films he plans to make when he gets home from school. He carries around a journal to record all the ideas he has for stories that he'll write and tell and film in the future. I know he's probably the spitting image of me when I was a kid, except I was a girl and had more internal motivation to keep things clean and tidy (although my mom would probably argue with me on that, based on the number of times she told me to clean my room as a teenager and I saw no problem with it in the first place). But he's got his daddy's absent-mindedness. I'll tell his daddy to grab a check as he's going out the door, and he'll forget three seconds later.

So it's not unusual to watch this boy bring a book downstairs that he's reading and then take it outside where his friends are playing, "just in case it gets a little boring" and then forget to pick it back up. As a result, I find books everywhere. I find them in the laundry basket, where they accidentally got picked up with some dirty clothes that some of the other boys left on the floor. I find them in the shoe storage baskets, when someone thought it would be funny to do an experiment and see if Brother's books will start to stink when living with shoes (Yes. They will. We now have a Harry Potter book that smells like old rotten corn chips). I'll find them in my room, on the coffee table, in the pantry where he stopped to get something to eat. I'll find them on the floor in their bathroom—which is revolting to me, considering how often they miss the toilet—and I'll find them resting in the pots of plants. I'll find them in the sink and beside the microwave. Everywhere.

We're always telling our boys to pick up after themselves, but I have a sneaking suspicion that for some it comes easier than for others. I'd venture to say that, in general, girls are more inclined to be neat and orderly. Maybe that's too much of a generalization. I am, after all, not a mother of girls. But I'm a girl, and I can say that even my limited neatness is leaps and bounds ahead of Husband's, and we've been married twelve years. Boys, it seems, do not come standard with the pick-up-after-yourself gene, as can be seen by spending a moment observing all the shoes scattered around my house and the toothbrushes that lie on the floor of their bathroom, which someone, when they slip away unnoticed, will "accidentally" dip in the pee water before someone else needs to brush his teeth. Even Husband can't be bothered to pick his clothes up off the floor. I trip over his shoes every other day. I try to find ways to be okay with all of this, but the truth is, I like to have a tidy, orderly house.

The messy one and I used to clash mightily about all of this, because every now and then I reach my capacity. Usually that happens when I allow myself to believe that maybe he's turned a corner, because we've had two days of no mess, two days of a boy putting things away without being asked. And then the earth will return to its normal tilt, and a book will be waiting on my bedside—a book I don't intend to read.

My messy child leaves random drawings of his characters all over the kitchen counter. He leaves his plans for today's Minecraft session on the dining room table. He leaves random questions that he wants to know the answers to on tiny slips of paper. He doesn't leave notes for me, even though I imagine that each of these left-out things is a love note to his mom.

What I'm really trying to say is that even though I don't want to be a maid for the rest of my life, I know that some kids have more trouble than others remembering to pick up after themselves. And because I don't want to be the mom who is constantly nagging her son at every step (I've tried. It's not fun.), I have to take things in stride. He'll learn, eventually. We've come a long way already. There's still a long way to go, but I'm confident that by the time he leaves my house, he will be able to remember that towels belong on the hook in the bathroom, not on the disgusting floor.

What I don't want is for my child to ever feel like there's something wrong with him just because he doesn't fit my expectation of who he should be. Sure, there will be consequences for leaving things all over the floor and table, but if those consequences are delivered with a look on my face that says he is annoying or inconvenient or maddening, I've gone too far. I know what it's like to feel like you were born disappointing, and it's not fun working through that kind of trauma when you're all the way grown.

So I've stopped nagging. I've started helping where I can, being his cheerleader, pointing out ways that might make it easier for him to keep a tidy room, brainstorming solutions that might help him remember things when he is lost in his own world. And I'm not going to take it personally the next time he leaves his bowl of oatmeal on the table.

There are way more important things than keeping a perfectly tidy home. And I don't want to miss a single one of them.

What it Means to Be a Boy: Compete in Everything

The other night one of our boys took out a game called Bounce Off and asked if we could play it once after-dinner chores were finished. I have trouble saying no to anything that is play happening anywhere that is not in front of a screen, so of course I agreed.

My older boys love playing this game, because it's one where you get to choose teams, and then you bounce a ball that has to land in a certain place on a board and make a pattern. It's challenging and active and enjoyable.

Well, it's enjoyable until one of them starts losing.

It didn't take long, this particular evening, for my 6-year-old to start crying about how he could never win, because he couldn't arrange his balls into the pattern he wanted.

I tried really hard not to roll my eyes.

I hear this familiar refrain often: "Aw, you're beating me." When I'm playing Go Fish with the 5-year-old, he is exceedingly happy that we're playing until he sees that I have three stacks of pairs while he only has one. The smile on his face slips. And then he'll get four pairs in a row and be beating me, and his smile will widen again. And then I'll get seven more pairs and there's no way for him to catch up, and he'll begin his sad, sad, song. "I wanted to win," he'll say.

"But we're still having fun, right?" I'll say.

"No," he'll say.

"You don't have fun unless you win?" I'll say.

He'll look at me like he thought his mama was smarter than this.

We were playing soccer recently out in the front yard of my mother's home, and the 6-year-old and I were on a team together, while the 9-year-old and his daddy were on a team. We were playing with no goalie, just all of us racing across a modified (as in, shorter) field. I already knew who was going to win, because if we'd had a soccer team at my high school, I would have played first string bench sitter. Sports are not my strong suit. Probably because I read too much as a kid.

So there I was, guarding their daddy, who has about fifty pounds on me and is an inch taller (but it's a big inch). He's also much quicker on his feet than I am (I blame the broken foot that happened a year ago—I'm still a little cautious about playing a game where my size 10 foot could get crushed by a men's size 13 one). The 6-year-old and I were doing okay at first, keeping a steady pace with Husband and Big Brother, and then I started getting a little tired, because, to be honest, I was pulling all the weight, since the 6-year-old hasn't learned how to properly pass or aim for a goal or, really, run. "I'm not that great at soccer," he said to me more than once, and, rather than encourage him, I said, "I'm not, either." I probably should have followed this up with a "You know that means we probably won't win, right? Let's just have fun playing." But I neglected those words, and I soon regretted it. His groan followed us back and forth across the field.

We started losing by more. Every time their daddy stole the ball from me, the 6-year-old would release a loud, inhuman growl-scream, because he knew that once his daddy got the ball, I wouldn't have enough speed to stop him (running isn't the same after you have six children. Trust me). I kept reminding my son that we were out here to have fun, not to win. That just made him cry more.

I suggested we should switch teams, but the 9-year-old didn't like this idea. He'd seen my skills, and he didn't want anything to do with them. The game quickly dissolved after that, because it wasn't much fun anymore.

Boys think it's important to win at everything. It doesn't matter what they're doing. They could be coloring two pictures that are completely different, but they want to win at coloring. They could be performing a play they've written, but they want to win at the acting. We might be having a dance party in the middle of our living room, and they want to win the dance, as if that's even possible when I'm around.

We play a game of kickball out in the yard, and they get mad when their daddy and I don't take it easy on them, because they want to win. When we're snuggling, they play with us a game of Uno, which is largely a game of chance, and they get mad that they didn't win one of the eight times we played. They race to school on mornings when it's not a thousand degrees outside by 7 a.m., and they want to win on the way up the hill, which means they'll do anything they can (pull each other down, trip each other, take the shortcut, even though I've lectured several times about poor sportsmanship and how cheaters don't technically win) to do it.

After the disastrous soccer game, Husband and I rounded up all the boys and took a walk through the cornfields. My parents live in the country, while we live in the city, and it's not often that our boys get to parade through farmlands and wilderness.

My stepdad practices his golfing technique in my parents' front yard. His balls land in random places in the cornfield and stick there, half submerged in the soil. The corn, at this time, had already been harvested, and we could see golf balls dotting the landscape. This gave the boys an idea: Let's collect all the golfballs.

This would have been a perfect plan, except the boys decided, of course, that they'd make it a competition, and the entire time, rather than having fun uncovering a golf ball, at least four of them were crying because they didn't make it to the golf ball first.

When I think about this phenomenon, I get it, kind of. I tend to be a competitive person and have to check myself when I'm playing board games with Husband, because it's really easy to get carried away with competition. It steals the fun out of things. No one wants to be the loser. The loser never thinks the game is fun in the end. And I'm mostly interested in my boys having fun, not putting all that pressure on themselves already. It's too early. They'll have plenty of that in life. They don't need it now, when they're young and it doesn't really matter.

So we try to teach them that sometimes you win and sometimes you lose. We try to teach them that you learn from losing—which doesn't mean you won't ever lose again, by the way. But it does mean an opportunity to make a plan for getting better, if that's really what you want to do. We try to teach them that life isn't really about winning or losing—it's about making the most of your journey and enjoying its twists and turns.

These concepts are much too complicated for them right now. And, honestly, when we're playing Ticket to Ride and Husband just laid down a track in the exact same place I was planning to lay down a track on my next turn, they're too complicated for my distraught mind, too. So I can almost understand the temptation to get bent out of shape over a silly game; it is maddening to lose.

But what I want my boys to understand is that losing says nothing about who we are. We are the same person after losing as we were before. And that's what really matters.

Win or lose, I want them to know they're always, always loved. And that's the only winning that matters, in the end.

Welcome to My Smelly Pit

The other night we were just settling down for dinner, and the 3-year-old sat in his chair, looking at us all, waiting for his turn to speak.

It's not often that the 3-year-old twins are given a chance to speak in our house, because there are a lot of people talking all the time—about school and Minecraft and Pokémon cards—but this time we could clearly see that he had something important to say, so we let him. And what he had to say was as profound and wonderful as you'd expect from a 3-year-old:

"I'm going to toot on the table," he said and then giggled.

Okay. So it wasn't at all profound and wonderful. But it did shed some light on circulating smells that were more potent than the actual salmon sprinkled with lemon on the table before us. It's not like this is something new, however. Boys bring with them many smells in a typical day.

I live in South Texas. That means that, for ten months out of the year, when boys go play outside, they will most definitely come back in smelling like a wet dog. They don't notice the smell, of course, because they don't really know what it means to smell bad. But I notice. I'm in the middle of cooking dinner, and it smells like a sheepdog that waded through a pool of sewage just stepped inside my kitchen. When I turn around, I see that it's not a sheepdog at all, it's the 5-year-old coming in for a drink of water before he races right back out into the sauna to sweat some more while flailing on the trampoline.

If we spend a day out on the town, where we walk around the historical streets of our city, visiting the Alamo and the Riverwalk and a local park and admiring all the horses pulling carriages, we will have to roll down the van windows on our way home, because the smell of our boys is much stronger than a horse pasture. The one who should be wearing deodorant doesn't see much use in it, so add to that horse-pasture smell a distinct and mighty body odor.

"What's that smell?" they'll say, and Husband and I will just laugh, because if there's anything that's impossible in the world, it's convincing boys that the smell that makes them wrinkle their noses is actually coming from them.

It's not just the smells they bring back in from outside, either. It's also the smells that happen throughout the course of a day. Ask any of them to take off their shoes, and you will pass out cold from the fumes that radiate from their socks. I know, because every laundry day I encounter those smelly socks and I have to wear a gas mask if I don't want to pass out and leave the fort to my 3-year-old twins.

Take a walk in their room, and you will think you are walking in an animal graveyard that didn't quite get the bodies buried before they started decomposing. This is likely because boys like to leave their dirty clothes—and especially their damp, dirty socks—under their beds.

Pass by their bathroom and you'd swear you were walking in a sewage dump. That's because boys hardly ever remember to flush the toilet and just let the yellow mellow into a distinctive and disgusting brown.

And then there's the massive amount of gas that's balled up inside their little frames. The volume of it is quite remarkable. It's not unusual for me to be reading a story and taking a deep and adequate breath so that I can properly mimic a man's voice, but, instead of breathing in clean air, I get a great big whiff of fart, and my nose hairs burn and the back of my throat closes up and I'm coughing it all out, because the invisible fumes that leaked out someone's cheeks are not air at all, they're poison to my lungs. The boys, naturally, are very proud of owning up to the fart, so we always know exactly who it was who let loose that SBD (Silent But Deadly), but when I tell them they need to hold it for another time and place, preferably when I'm nowhere around, their daddy will interject a comment about how it's really bad for you to hold farts and it could cause all sorts of problems later. To which I'll respond, "That's fine, but make your bathroom the gas chamber, not this library. I would like to live." To which they then reply that it would be impossible to make it to the bathroom before the gas slipped out.

It's hilariously funny for them to let loose an SBD when we're in the car with all the windows up and the air conditioning turned on high and suddenly we're all choking and waving our hands in front of our faces because something crawled up inside someone and died and then crawled back out their fart flappers. They bust out laughing every time one of these farts makes a noise other than what is typical —like "pat" or "pop" or the whine kind, and then they'll keep trying to do it until they have to run off to the bathroom because they tried a little too hard.

The other night I was coming in to check on my 9-year-old in the bath tub, because it was about time for him to dry off and get out so we could start story time, and I knew he wouldn't want to miss the chapter book we're reading. I got to my room, which is where he bathes, since we only have two bathtubs and when you have six kids you have to stagger the bathing, and I could have sworn there was a motorboat in the water. When I poked my head in, he was laughing to himself, and the first thing he said, upon seeing me, was "Do you smell it?" I hightailed it out of there, because not only did I not want to smell it, but it was also my bathroom he was making his mark in. I came back a few minutes later to tell him it was time to get out, for real, and he was passed out in the tub.

Not really. But it probably could have happened if the bathroom door had been closed instead of wide open, because the smell, thankfully, dissipated into my room. I know, because when I pulled back the covers of my bed, there was a great rush of heat that smelled like someone had dissected a bunghole and put the pile of whatever was inside it beneath my covers, especially for me. The smell was trapped in the fibers, I think.

Husband says I'm wrong about that. He says it was actually me.

Well, I don't like to argue about technicalities. I don't find it necessary to always be right, like some people do.

The smells that boys bring to a home can be an inconvenience when you have guests coming over to visit, but they're, right now, easily hidden by the spritz of essential oil and a little strategic positioning of the diffusers. I realize that when they get older, my house will probably smell like a locker room, but we've got a little time between now and then. I'm confident that I'll figure out a solution.

Or maybe I'll just have to get used to it, because this is life with boys.

The Bumpy Handoff of a Grandparents Weekend

My boys are fortunate to have two sets of grandparents who live in Texas. Their grandparents every now and then offer to keep them, in shifts, for the weekend, and they'll take our boys all sorts of fun places and load them with sugar and feed them all the foods they're not allowed to have in our house. They'll let them stay up too late and deal with their whininess the next morning and effectively dismantle the schedule we sent them as a suggestion and then, two days later, hand them back to us with their eyes twitching.

"Here," they'll say. "You can have them back now."

"You don't want them for a couple more days?" we'll say hopefully.

"Maybe next time," they'll say.

And we know there won't be more days next time, because you know what? Raising six boys (even watching them for a couple of days) is *really hard work.*

On the way home from picking the kids up from the grandparents, the kids will typically tell us, in halting and never-ending fashion, about all the awesome food they had, which had sugar counts I don't really want to know, and then they will, without even taking a breath, move on to all the fun things they did, like going to play golf and watching a movie every single night and swimming in a pool and swinging on a tire swing or digging in the huge dirt piles in their grandparents' front yard and sleeping in their clothes instead of their pajamas and taking a bath all by themselves and having donuts for breakfast and going out to eat pizza and wearing their brother's clothes instead of their own because grandparents don't usually check labels and so don't see that this crop-top belongs to the 3-year-old and not the 6-year-old.

Usually, while the boys are gone, Husband and I will work hard to clean up our house, which means that when we get home, the boys walk into a perfectly tidy, perfectly ordered house. Two minutes (or fewer) later, they will pull out all the stacks of artwork they did at their grandparents' house and scatter the papers all over the floor because they think we surely want to see it all, even though it's nothing new that we haven't already seen. They'll ask for dinner and go raid the fridge when we answer that it'll be coming soon, and then they'll have their first meltdown because there's nothing good to eat in this house—at least nothing that compares to Lucky Charms and donuts and McDonalds and anything else that makes me sick just thinking about.

After this meltdown, they'll progress into talking about how we're the worst parents ever, because we never let them watch a movie or stay up too late or have donuts for breakfast, and we start going out of our minds trying to follow behind them and fix all the things they're destroying as they're walking around bemoaning the state of their life. We'd really like to start Monday with a clean house, but kids would really like to take that possibility and rip it into tiny little pieces we can't see anymore.

We'll move into the unpacking mode, splitting the shift where one of us unpacks and the other cooks dinner, but you'll notice that both of these jobs leave few eyes to watch the melting down, tornado-like children. Dinner will be the worst dinner they've ever tasted, baths will be the worst time they've ever had in the bath, bed time will be the worst thing they've ever experienced in all their lives, and by the time the evening is finished, we will be the Worst Parents Ever.

There is definitely a detox time when it comes to handing off children to grandparents and then taking them back. We will have to detox their food expectations, their sleep expectations, their complete and utter lack of routine. We will probably be driven near out of our minds in the process. This adjustment period makes life feel like it will never be the same again. But eventually it will even out. And I will eventually be thankful that we took a weekend away and the boys got to have an opportunity to spend time with their grandparents for a couple of days.

On the surface, it might seem that the only reason a parent would want to send kids away with grandparents is to get a break themselves. And this is definitely one of the great perks of grandparent weekends. Husband and I have used our weekends to talk and actually finish a sentence. We've used them to cook dinners together that no one will complain about (although we usually have enough leftovers for an army, because we don't know how to cook for two people anymore). We've used them to reconnect, dream, work, sightsee, and share a cup of coffee without a kid climbing on our laps (that's not to say I don't thoroughly enjoy my kids climbing onto my lap. I do. It hardly ever happens anymore, because no one ever wants to sit still anymore).

But what grandparent weekends also do is give two completely different generations an opportunity to get to know each other.

Grandparents don't have the burden of discipline like they did when they were raising their own children. They get to be fun. They get to be doting. They get to be the rule relaxers. This keeps them young—it's been proven by science. Grandparents who take an active role in their grandchildren's lives have sharper brains, more capable bodies, and greater heart health. (Keep that in mind, Mom.)

And kids get to experience their own benefits. It's important that kids interact with another generation that is removed from their parents' generation, because they can learn important things from their wisdom (like how you actually should wear deodorant when you turn ten). Kids get to experience the unconditional love of a grandparent who is not quite as concerned as their parents are over who they might turn out to be—because time has given grandparents perspective, and they know that everything irons out eventually. Kids get to be kids without someone continuously harping on them about picking up their dirty socks.

So while I start to dread the hand-off from a Grandparents Weekend about halfway into that freedom, I'm glad every single time that we sent the kids away perfectly calm and controlled and pick them back up crazy little wildings who forget what it means to brush their teeth and put away their clothes and do such things as after-dinner chores. I'm glad, because I know it's all for everyone's good.

My kids are currently climbing up the walls with their toe-knuckles. I'm currently scheduling the next Grandparents Weekend.

How Boys Fight: Incessantly

I was not a physical child. Some might say this is most likely because I was a girl, but I also didn't get angry all that often—at least not angry enough to hit. I do remember hitting my sister once and only once, when we were teenagers and she said something that really enraged me. I think it had been piling for a while. She stole one of my shirts, messed it up, and tried to hide it from me. It was something really important like that.

It's an entirely different story with my boys. My boys can pick a fight and finish it before I can even get the words, "We touch each other gently" out of my mouth. One minute one of them is complaining about how his brother stole a piece of his puzzle, and the next minute the words are knocked out of his mouth by an errant smack (not by me. I don't hit my kids. Neither does Husband. That shows us that this is something that is born inside them.). Of course they get in trouble for this. Of course they have to make amends when they're ready (I don't like insincere amends). Of course there are consequences intended to keep them from doing it again. But it never works.

I've heard stories from other parents of boys who say that their kids, even when they were teenagers, didn't get over this physical part of their nature. Husband tells me a story from his childhood wherein his parents weren't home and he and his brother, 15 and 13, respectively, started fist-fighting because they could not agree on something also really important, like who left the light on. Husband punched his brother, and his brother started crying and writhing on the floor like it really hurt, but when Husband came close to make sure his brother was really okay, his brother punched him right in the face. Husband responded by locking his brother outside the house and not letting him in no matter what or how loud or how long he screamed. This is a lovely thing to look forward to.

For the life of me, I can't understand this immediate physical response. When I feel angry, I don't see a wall and think, *I should hit that.* I might see the wall and think that I would like to hit it because I feel so angry inside that hitting might make me feel better. But then there's this complicated thought process that happens after that initial observation, and I'm suddenly thinking about how much it would hurt to hit a wall and how I'd most likely break something, and I really don't want to break something, because I need my hands for writing and for playing the bass guitar and for picking up my youngest son, and then I start thinking about what I would possibly do if I broke my hand, and the answer is, I would go a little crazy, because things would pretty much fall apart in a home like ours. One parent down is like claiming defeat before the battle has even begun. How would I cook? How would I do my workout? How would I keep the boys out of anything, when I would have only one hand and already need fifteen? So the thought, *I should hit a wall,* never results in an action.

The problem is that boys don't have this complicated thought process. They just receive the thought, *I should hit that,* and they do it. I know, because the 9-year-old has done it before. He's hit a cabinet or a table or something else—more than once, I should add

—and every time he crumples up like his hand is undergoing the worst pain imaginable. Tell me why you would do this again. He always regrets it.

I also know this because Husband punched a wall when a picture dropped down and cut the top of his skull, and the nerve of something this ridiculous happening sent him over the edge for a brief moment in time. He put a hole in the dining room wall.

I know, too, because the 6-year-old, who is one of the kindest children you will ever meet in your life, has hit his little brothers when they destroyed his writing journal and he couldn't make sense of the masterful pages after they got finished with it.

Boys hit. They don't think.

We've tried to create a system that will help them think before they do anything. Emotions are tough, and the moments of emotional flood are even tougher. We have reminders for them to breathe. We have consequences. We have rewards.

I'm beginning to think that systems don't work.

When our boys hit one another, they'll do their brother's chores to make up for it—washing the dishes, taking out the trash, cleaning up the toys they were playing with alone instead of together. They will be required to write a kind note to their wounded brother. They will be expected to complete their retribution—sincerely.

And yet often I wonder if there is something within them that is simply wired to be physical. Brain science hints that there is, of course. But even if brain science wasn't around to suggest this, one could take a look at a boy's play pattern. My boys will regularly roll on the ground and wrestle each other until someone is crying in mercy. They enjoy standing up at the top of our stairs while Husband throws heavy couch pillows at them and tries to knock them down. They think it's fun to engage in a slap-fight.

One time, when we lingered a little longer than usual at the library playground, our boys were playing with some other boys they'd found somewhere around the slides. The 9-year-old hurtled past me, screaming for his life. I thought he might be hurt, so I followed him. It was not easy to catch him, but I eventually did.

"Hey," I said. "Are you okay? I couldn't tell if you were upset or happy."

"We're playing a game," he said and made as though to move off again. I grabbed his arm.

"What kind of game?" I said.

"A hitting game," he said.

"What?" I said. "Why would you want to play a hitting game?"

"Because it's fun," he said.

"That is not my definition of fun," I said.

He laughed and said, "That's because you're a girl, Mama." And he ran off.

On the way home, I listened to the chatter in the back seat. All three of my older boys miraculously agreed on something: They couldn't wait to play the Hit Until You Cry game again.

The Delight of an Early Saturday Morning

Every school morning, at exactly 6:30, I walk into my boys' treacherously messy room, touch them on their shoulders, and say, "It's time to get up for school!" in a decidedly cheerful (and probably slightly annoying) voice. Every morning they complain about how early it is and how I should let them sleep for longer and how they should change the start time for school so they can stay in bed later.

Some mornings we'll go through a whole routine where one of them will pretend to be sick, and I'll feel his forehead and there's no fever. Another will chime in that he doesn't want to go to school and thinks he's going to throw up. He'll hang over the disgusting toilet, which, in my opinion, shows some initiative (it's really very disgusting). Nothing comes out either end, though.

And still another (who hasn't even climbed out of bed yet) will say that he can't find his backpack or his folder, or, worse, his shoes, so he guesses that means he'll just have to stay home today, because, of course, all of those are things he absolutely cannot go to school without, because his teacher would hate him. (He's a little melodramatic.)

I get it. It's really hard to get out of bed that early in the morning, and elementary schools probably should start a little later in the day so kids could get a little more sleep. The bedtime in our house is 8:15 p.m., but the problem is that boys aren't even tired yet, so they'll lie in bed talking to each other or laughing at jokes or imagining shapes in the darkness.

Still, it's a great mystery to me that when Saturday rolls around and my boys have a wide open day to sleep late, they're out of bed by 5:30 a.m.

Now. This wouldn't be such a bad thing if Husband and I kept the same schedule on a Saturday morning as we do all the other mornings. On school days, we're typically out of bed at 4:15, because that's what time you have to get yourself out of bed in order to have a little time to yourself before all the kids and the craziness of a school morning unleash havoc on you. If you're me, I mean. And you have six children. Who talk all over each other in the mornings and you reach overwhelm capacity two minutes after they wake up.

I usually have a little writing time and reading time and then I get breakfast ready and have their vitamins and drinks all neatly arranged in their places at the table. I'll sign folders and stack their school things that need to be packed and then I'll quietly ascend the stairs to wake them all with my soothing voice. In other words, I have a routine.

But on Friday nights, Husband and I usually have a fake date at home, because it's hard to get a sitter when you have six kids. We'll stay up way too late watching a movie or a Netflix series and hanging out together. Sometimes we record some things that we can't record when kids are awake and shaking the walls down. And then, after all that, I usually stay up for a little bit longer to get some reading done, which rarely happens anymore (actually that's not true. I'm very protective of my reading time.). And then, finally, we'll go to bed, thinking that this midnight bedtime—or sometimes even later than that—will not adversely affect us at all, because the kids will surely not be out of bed before 7:30 or so.

This is a good example of Delusional Thinking.

Parents are pretty good at Delusional Thinking.

It never unfolds this way. The boys, see, are faced with this wide open space of time, and they think that means they must wring every possible minute out of it. They must rise at the earliest hour they can rise—sometimes at 5 a.m., if we're really lucky. They must then, because there are no parents around, take out everything they can possibly hope to play with on this day off—Uno, Go Fish, every LEGO piece container we own. Around 6 or so they start realizing that they're dying of hunger, so they'll bust into our room. We'll fly from the bed because we have good reflexes in the case that this intruder has malicious intent, take note in our foggy brain that it's our child, look at the window, which indicates the sun has not yet risen, and sigh. Loudly.

"I'm so hungry," they'll say. "What's for breakfast?"

"Nothing until 7," is our usual response.

"What time is it?" they'll say.

"Time for you to get a watch," Husband will say, because he doesn't lose his sense of humor even in the fog of weariness.

Someone will groan (probably me). Someone else will growl (probably the intruder). Husband will tell them: "It's 6. You have an hour." Someone will groan again (probably the intruder). Someone else will growl (I don't know who that one is).

If they don't say anything when they burst into our room, it's usually because they're about to launch themselves toward our bed, and then we'll have an early breakfast of knees and elbows and—best of all—toes. Our faces will quickly be trapped beneath behinds.

We'll shove them away, and someone will inevitably get hurt.

On the very rare Saturday morning, one of them might climb into bed with us. These are my favorite mornings, even though boys squirm and wiggle. They're getting older, and they don't often come snuggle with us anymore, but we'll take advantage of every opportunity we have. I don't mind the intrusion when it comes with a sweet snuggle.

The moment, of course, is quickly broken by a "Why do you take up so much space in the bed, Mama?"

Never am I reminded how many elbows, knees, behinds, and mouths exist in my house than on a Saturday morning.

I remember waking up early on Saturday mornings when I was a kid, too. The difference was that my mom stuck me in front of Saturday morning cartoons. We don't even keep a television out where the boys can reach it. And, even if we did, they'd fight over what to watch. We know because it happens every Friday night for Family Movie Night. We don't need someone bursting into our room with a bleeding nose.

As inconvenient as it is, I guess I'll just have to get used to my boys waking before the sun on Saturday mornings, even though it's my only day to sleep late, because I don't trust them for more than a half hour without parental supervision. I'm not a big fan of the whole house burning down around me.

I know that one of these days they'll be teenagers and then it will be a daily challenge to get them out of bed even if it's a weekend. I know they'll retreat into themselves and hardly even talk to us. I know that snuggling with Mama and Daddy will likely not even cross their minds.

So, for now, I'll enjoy the early mornings of constant fighting, constant mess, and constant chatter. I'd rather have a way-too-early-in-the-morning house than a sleeping-the-day-away one.

At least until this Saturday rolls around.

The Cloud of Dirt that Follows Boys Around

To the people who ask me what it's like raising six boys, I usually answer "It's like raising six Pig Pens." Remember that character from Charlie Brown who always walked around with a dirt cloud following him? That's Pig Pen. And he's the definition of a boy.

My boys will be out playing in a pool, and they will come back home with dirt streaked across their faces. They will be taking a bath, and they'll get out with dirt clumped in their hair. They will be sleeping and wake up with dirt on their feet. Boys attract dirt. It leaks from their pores.

The other day, my twins wanted to go play outside. I'm fine with this—in fact, I'm more than fine with this, because when they play outside it allows me a moment to myself, which I'll likely use to clean something. I told them to stay on the back deck, however, because it was raining. Every few minutes, I looked out the window to make sure they were following my instructions, because these two can move lightning-fast when they realize that there is no parent watching. But they were, for once, following instructions amazingly well.

And then I called them in. They walked in with mud all over their faces.

"Where did you find mud?" I said. I was perplexed, because I hadn't seen them step off the deck.

"Outside," they said.

"On the deck?" I said.

They nodded.

And, sure enough, someone had left a bucket full of mud from the backyard hole they're digging in an effort to make a journey to the center of the earth. My twins found that bucket of mud and decided it looked like something good to eat (in an ironic turn of events, these guys have never been sick, even though they've eaten dirt many, many times. I'm starting to think maybe I should eat dirt.).

It doesn't matter where we go or what we're doing, my boys will still manage to find every patch of dirt they can. They will find dirt in the bathtub (usually the dirt crumbling off them). They will find dirt in the corners of my house (Wait. That's because I haven't cleaned in way too long). They will find dirt in the car and at the children's museum and inside a public bathroom.

Parents of boys will notice that not only are boys Pig Pens, but their houses become pigpens—as in the places where pigs sleep, not the character from Charlie Brown—as well. Because boys carry dirt in every crevice, they will leave that dirt everywhere. Clouds of dirt follow them, like little sand tornadoes. They peel their dirty clothes off their bodies as soon as they walk in the door from school, and dirt showers around them. They'll head outside topless and, before too long, bring in some snails from the Great Outdoors, along with some roly polies, a few salamanders, and, of course, very large spiders. They'll bring in acorns with acorn weevils that will hatch in our banana basket. They'll bring in filthy sticks they'll use as magic wands. They'll bring in ziplock bags of nothing but dirt because they thought I'd like it as a gift. Thanks, but no thanks.

It's not just the dirt that follows them everywhere. It's also the mess. When we're reading in our home library, there will suddenly be a billion books on the floor, and not one of them is responsible for this disaster. Their room will be completely spotless for half a second and then you turn around to tell your husband to come look, and when he does there's a LEGO piece explosion all over the floor. You can do something nice for them and pick up their stinky soccer socks, and there will be another pair on the ground, pronto.

My boys are probably the messiest people in my house. It doesn't help that two of them are twins and daily conspire to turn our house inside out and rough around the edges. They are currently going through their three hundredth annoying stage wherein they empty their closet of everything in it and then pretend like there will be no repercussions for this senseless act of savagery. When Husband or I walk in to get them from their naps, they will pretend like they don't even notice the clothes all over the floor. They will walk out like they own the world, and then they'll spend the next hour hanging everything up before they can come play, because consequences. It doesn't matter that they don't know how to hang clothes on hangers. They'll stay in their rooms until they figure out how—because while they might have gotten a pass the first couple of times, they did not deserve a pass for the next fifty times.

My point is that it's impossible to keep up with these six Pig Pens in my house. I've pretty much stopped trying. I haven't stopped hoping, though, and I definitely haven't stopped nagging, because some things never die. But no matter how much nagging I manage to do, there will be marks on the walls from all the dirt boys bring inside. There will be dirt streaks on the ceiling that I'll wonder how in the world got there (Answer: A muddy shoe that was kicked straight up in the air. Glad we could figure that one out.). There will be dirt caked on the bottom of my bath tub, because we only have two bathtubs, and six boys in one tub is too much. And six boys taking individual baths is also too much. So I have to share.

There will be dirt on their clothes, even after I'm done washing them, which means there will also be dirt in the bottom of the washing machine that will need its own cycle sans clothes to clean. It means my bed will have a layer of dirt on it, since that's where I fold the clothes. It means that their room will become a sand box, because clothes will remain on the floor to be walked on, slept on, and, when laundry day comes back around, tossed in the hamper.

Living with Pig Pens is no small accomplishment. In fact, I consider it one of my greatest. I do, after all, still maintain a sliver of my sanity, after living so long completely outnumbered.

The only problem I see is that now a cloud of dirt follows me everywhere, too. I guess you can't parent boys without being utterly changed.

The Looking Limitations of Boys

"I've looked and looked and looked. Where could it be?"

It's been three mornings of the same thing—he climbs out of bed late and almost misses breakfast, because there are LEGO pieces all over the floor and he can't walk past them without building a miniature version of San Antonio's Alamo. He'll turn on an audio book, stretch out on the floor, and listen and build.

The problem is that there's a deadline on mornings. This isn't the case when school's out, but it's only the one-hundredth day of school, and so we still have another two hundred or so to go—which would make one think, if one were as gullible as I am—that maybe we would have gotten the hang of this by now.

Nope.

So there he is, playing with LEGO figures when there's still a backpack to be packed, a lunch to be put together, shoes to be located. And the best part about it is he's not very good at looking.

Yesterday morning he couldn't find his shoes that were sitting under his desk, where he slipped them off while he was writing a thesis the other day (not really a thesis. But this particular boy will be well practiced at writing theses by the time he gets to college). He says one of his brothers probably shoved them under his desk as a joke, because he specifically remembers putting them where shoes go ("Where do shoes go?" I said. He just looked at me blankly, so, yeah, I think he's telling the truth.).

Yesterday afternoon he couldn't find the digital camera he got for Christmas to use in his filmmaking endeavors, and he ranted all over the house about how someone had taken it or stolen it or misplaced it (but that person was most definitely not him), and then when we found it on the table beside the couch, he, of course, had not put it there.

Last night he couldn't find the soap container that was sitting on the edge of the bath tub, where it always is.

Today he can't find his jacket. It's right in the middle of the floor.

Once a week he can't find a library book that someone—one of his brothers, probably—surely must have hidden on purpose. He can't find this one specific LEGO piece, because they've all exploded on the floor and one looks so like another, but, actually, someone probably lost it (not him). He can't find the CD player that's still spinning because no one ever wants to press stop, only pause ("Can't you hear the clicking, son?" "What clicking?"), which is hidden beneath the clothes he stripped off yesterday and left on the floor, because that's where they belong. He can't find his favorite Star Wars shirt because putting his clothes away after laundry day means stuffing them all into his drawers, instead of hanging them in his closet (one of these days, when he actually cares about the way he looks, he'll realize that the "homeless" look isn't all that compelling in the eyes of a young lady).

And it's not just him. The rest of them got this not-great-at-looking gene, too.

"Where's my scarf?" the 4-year-old says.

"It's hanging around your neck," I say.

"Where's my backpack?" the 5-year-old says.

"It's on the chair right behind you, where you laid it," I say.

"Where's Daddy?" one of the 2-year-olds says.

"You're looking right at him," I say. "How is it that you can't see him?"

Kids just aren't all that great at looking.

Husband would say they get this from me. "Have you seen my water?" I'll say, and he'll point to the banister in front of me, the most unlikely of places, which suddenly reminds me that I put it there a few minutes ago.

"Do you have the other keys?" he'll say when we're walking out the door. I'll check my purse. "No," I'll say. He'll look at me. And then he'll pull my purse away from me, because clearly I'm incompetent at looking, and I'll roll my eyes and mutter under my breath, "You're not going to find anything. I'd be able to hear them," and then out he'll pull them. I have no idea how they got there.

"I can't find his red folder," I'll say about the one boy missing a school folder.

"Did you look?" Husband will say, his voice muffled against the pillow because it's still 6 a.m. and he likes getting up early.

"Yes," I'll say. "And he needs it today. There are important papers that need to go back to school."

Husband will rouse himself from the bed and rifle through the billions of papers on our counter and miraculously find it at the bottom of the stack, where I swear it must have reappeared in the time between walking upstairs and now.

My Pride and Prejudice bag? I'll say.

Probably in the closet, where it should be, Husband will say.

The sour cream? I'll say.

Right in front of your face, he'll say, grabbing it from the shelf that's not actually right in front of my face but is more level with my forehead and above my line of sight.

My running shoes?

Downstairs in the basket, where they're supposed to be.

Every now and then Husband will lose his wallet, and I'll do a quick glance around the room, not see it anywhere, and already be on the phone with the credit card companies to cancel the two we carry, and he'll walk back in the room with the wallet he found on the windowsill behind our blinds, where I wouldn't even think to look (and why would I? What's it doing *there*?).

I'm not entirely sure where this aversion to looking comes from. I blame it on the kids. I think I'm so overwhelmed with looking for things all the time that I just suffer from a condition called Looking Burnout, so when there's something right in front of my face I don't actually see it. One of the many hazards of having kids.

But something needs to be done about these kids and their sadly lagging looking skills. I'm not a find-this-for-me service. I'm not even a find-this-for-myself service, as you can see from the stories I've shared. So, eventually, someone is going to have to teach my kids how to properly look for something, and it's most likely not going to be me. Which means it will probably fall to Husband.

Hey, you know what? We all have our own strengths. That's part of what makes community important.

Now where did I put my computer?

I See London, I See France, Go Put on Some Underpants

Last night I dressed my 10-month-old in Star Wars pajamas and set him in a little kid chair, and I snapped a picture of him, because he was so happy and it was so stinking cute. And then I posted the picture on my social media sites today, because, like I said, it was cute, and everybody loves cute photos of babies, and sometimes all we need to feel like we're on top of a Monday is to see the smiling face of a cute, happy baby. But all was not as it should have been.

I did not check the picture for surprise appendages. Maybe it's because I've gotten so used to ignoring the naked parts that go flying around my house. I live with a tribe of boys, after all, who would, hands down, prefer no clothes to clothes any hour of any day. After so much of all that nakedness, you just become immune to it.

Another boy mom noticed and sent me a message saying I had an unintended addition in the corner of the picture. So I took it down, cropped it and put it back up. Because it really was a great picture.

It probably goes without saying that I cannot "just snap" a picture in my home, because there is always a little boy running straight out of the bathroom without the pants he had on two seconds ago. I can't "just take a quick video" of my boys dancing to "What Does the Fox Say" (which is still highly popular in our house), because one of them will get too hot and strip down to nothing but his birthday suit. I can't just open the door to see who rang the bell, because it's guaranteed that someone will peek around the corner, even though I told him to stay in his seat, showing more parts than he should.

Lately we've been the hub of the neighborhood. Kids like to come to our house, because we're super cool parents. Actually, it's more likely because we have a trampoline and a swing set in our backyard and we let the kids play in freedom unless someone is dying. But this becoming a hub also means that at all hours of the day we have kids knocking on our door, asking to play.

On Saturday, I opened the door to find a little curly-haired girl. "I came over to play," she said, walking right in before I could stop her. Problem is, we'd just gotten up, and when boys have just gotten up, there's no guarantee that they are dressed in anything at all, because there is some sort of clothes bandit who keeps stealing into our house and stealing out of it with the pajamas my boys were wearing when we kissed them goodnight. I couldn't be sure what exactly the situation was as I peered from the living room into the kitchen, because they were all wrapped in their blankets, since it was a cold morning. But then the 9-year-old stood up to go to the bathroom, dropping the wrapped-around-him blanket, and all he had on was fluorescent green boxers. At least he had something on, I guess.

But that little girl saw more than she probably should have. (Well. You probably shouldn't ring our doorbell at 7 a.m. on a Saturday and then walk right in as if you own the place. So. Lesson learned. Hopefully.)

Will I ever get to a place where I can "just snap" a picture or "just take a quick video" or just answer the door? I don't know. I do know that I have had to put some rules in place that I never, ever thought I would have to put in place back before I became a boy mom.

They sound a little like this:

Anyone who doesn't at least have underwear at the table doesn't get any food.

Absolutely no one may go outside in only their underwear (even in the fenced backyard).

Do not dance naked through the living room.

Because, you know, sometimes people knock on the door, and they don't want to see your pride and joy. And sometimes people are out mowing their lawn while you're jumping on the trampoline in your Captain America butt huggers, and they don't want to see an accidental slip. And sometimes we forget to close the blinds, and people don't want to see a streaker when they've only just woken up.

And, more importantly, sometimes Mama just wants to take a picture. For the love, go put on some underpants.

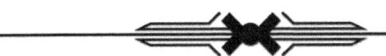

Growing Up is Hard to Do

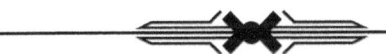

When the Magic of Mama's Kiss Fades Away

There is only one boy in my house who wants me to kiss the hurts away, and he is the youngest.

I remember a time when my boys would get hurt, and they would come clambering into my room or into my office space asking for a kiss to make something better. I used to do it for the twins all the time, because usually when one would get hurt and see that Mama had kissed away that pain, the other would remember an unrelated hurt, from days ago, that still needed kissing.

Mama's kisses used to be magic, but that goes away right around the age of 4.

The other day my youngest was trying to get off the couch, and usually he does it the right way, so I didn't feel the need to spot him. He masters this climb nine times out of ten. I figure that's pretty good odds. Unfortunately, this happened to be the one time out of ten, and he went rolling off the couch onto the carpeted floor, which we've been talking about tearing out and turning into a stained concrete floor. But after the youngest bumped his head and ended up with an impressive rug burn, I think we'll hold off for a while.

He came to me with his little red mark on the top of his forehead, big fat tears rolling down his chunky cheeks. When I picked him up, he stuck his forehead right against my mouth. I kissed it, because this is our ritual, and who knows how long it will last? For now, he gets hurt, he brings the hurt to me so I can kiss it away. And it works like magic every time. He'll move away and play again, seeming to have forgotten all about whatever was hurting him in the first place. And I never cease to marvel that he's been healed just because of a little imagination.

I possessed this magical ability for a time with all of my boys. They used to all come to me, some more than others, because they believed that my kisses were magical. There's something special about a little boy or a little girl (I don't even know if they do it, because I've never had the experience of raising a little girl) believing fully in the healing properties of a mama's kiss. Because the thing is, I always want to kiss away their hurts, even though one is nine and another is seven and another is six and two others are four and the last one almost two. I always want to kiss away their hurts, even when it gets as complicated as a little girl breaking their heart. Even when it's as complicated as someone doing something terrible to them or the loss of a friend or making a bad grade on a test. I want to order their worlds just so, take away all that pressing pain and help them go through life with ease and comfort.

I've been thinking about this often lately. I didn't have an easy childhood. I grew up on the edge of poverty. I knew what it was like to go to bed hungry, and it wasn't my mother's fault. She was raising three kids on her own, after my dad left when I was 11. I had to deal with parental divorce, and it broke me. I had to deal with a father who left for good and didn't even try to keep in touch. And there were places that shredded in me. I don't ever, ever want my children to feel that kind of pain.

Because I'm so sensitive to causing any kind of pain in my children, sometimes I beat myself up when I lose my temper and yell at my kids. But what it always comes back to is this: a little difficulty is good for kids. How else will they learn resilience if they don't ever have to face the hard parts of a life? How will they ever figure out that never giving up is the only option in succeeding? If we order their lives just so, if we're the perfect parents all the time—always patient, always calm, always completely and utterly adoring—how will they learn how to bounce back from the challenges in their lives?

We give them a safe place to explore challenge and perseverance.

The challenge in my own childhood is an extreme example. But I am grateful for it all the same. It has given me an understanding of others like me. It has given me wisdom on how to heal, how to be more human, how to prevent the same mistakes in my own life. It has shown me how far I've come.

I can teach my kids all day long about perseverance and what it's like to overcome something difficult—because we can do hard things—and what it's like to choose to love someone even though they're being incredibly difficult and inconvenient, but the only way they're going to really learn it is by experiencing it themselves.

I'm not saying that we should go out and try to make life difficult for our kids—although they'll likely, at least for a time, say that's what our sole mission in life is. That wouldn't serve them, either. They want parents who are on their side, and as much as we can, we should be. But we can't simply arrange their lives in order to protect them from every hurt that will come hurtling their way. We can't beat ourselves up for the bad decisions and mistakes that we make over the years, because it's all developing character in their lives. They get to see, by our imperfect lives, that they are growing up in an imperfect world, and they will need skills to survive that imperfection.

The other day, my 7-year-old came home with a paper that he had done in class, and it was some of that crazy math that I don't even know how to do, even though I aced high school calculus and college algebra. The way the questions were worded, however, were confusing. He could not figure out what the question was asking, and neither could I. And I felt indignant for him, because he'd made a bad grade even though he tried really hard to answer them in the way he thought they were supposed to be answered.

I momentarily thought about writing a letter to his teacher, but I didn't, because what he can learn from accepting that bad grade and knowing that he is worth more than his grades is something far more important than the triumph of acing every worksheet.

So I told him the truth: it wasn't a big deal, he would do better next time, and the grade didn't change who he was. He smiled at me so widely I melted into a puddle on the ground.

Sometimes all our children need to know is that they are capable of overcoming.

Good thing childhood gives them plenty of opportunities to absorb that truth. Our magic kiss.

This is the Last Time: Words that Bring Heartache

I've reached the point in my pregnancy when I no longer enjoy it, when I start trying every trick in the book to induce labor, when I can't wait a second longer to meet the little one who's keeping me up late again.

Every step feels like it might be my last, sleeping has gone the way of Pokémon Go (here today, gone tomorrow), and just sitting makes my back feel like it's been masquerading as a piñata for some over-jubilant 4-year-olds. I can't wait to be done.

And then I remember my done is DONE.

It's a finish I haven't been able to do. Last baby. Last pregnancy. Last gleam in a daddy's eye and hope in a mama's heart.

We waited two years after twins, because twins were so incredibly hard (and still are, by the way), and then we said one more, and we knew this was it, this was the last one, this would be the period at the end of our family's sentence.

And here I am, in the last week of my last pregnancy, and I get choked up every time I think about it.

It's right. I know that. It's what is best for our family, what is best for me, what is best for all my boys.

It's just that an ending doesn't ever feel easy, and this is an ending of the hardest sort—an ending of childbearing, an ending of welcoming a new life, an ending of giving over my life to something greater than me.

"Soak up your last week pregnant," my cousin said to me, and I swallowed the lump in my throat.

So I do.

This is the last time I will feel a baby stretch and move inside me, the last time I will get to know a tiny person before any of his family does, the last time my organs will shift and move aside for new life.

This is the last time I will eat key lime pie because a baby demanded it.

This is the last time I will wear those stretchy clothes and walk outside in slippers, because it's all about comfort now.

This is the last time I will get stuck on my back trying to turn over.

This is the last time I will put my hands on my belly and imagine what this one will look like—blue-eyed or brown-eyed?

This is the last time I will carry a load of laundry down the stairs with a back screaming curses and a frontside threatening to topple me over.

This is the last time I will waddle to the car and bite my lip against discomfort and pain and the things I want to say to my husband, who is humming in the driver's seat because he has not a care in the world about what's waiting in a labor and delivery ward.

This is the last time I will feel a contraction tightening my belly, splitting my muscles, doing its intended work.

This is the last time I will let those ice chips melt in a cup beside my labor bed and drink the water that pools at the bottom.

This is the last time I will hold my husband's hand through the pain and wave of drugs or no drugs.

This is the last time I will ache and groan and push new life, new hope, into the world.

This is the last time I will look on a newborn face and know that he is love, that he is mine.

This is the last time I will watch my beautiful boys kiss their new baby brother.

This is the last time I will work so hard to get my body back.

This is the last time I will make room in my home and my heart for another little one.

There will be other lasts, too. The last time I will wait for the word *Mama*, the last time I will wait for those heart-ripping ones, *I love you*, the last time I will get a misaimed slobbery kiss from another boy who has stolen my heart.

This whole year, his whole life, will be a series of lasts.

But I won't think of that just now. I will think only of this moment, one of the lasts, when the kicks of his feet rippling my belly tell me he'll be just like his brothers: curious, active, and persistent.

I can't wait to meet him.

They Hold My Heart in Their Hands

It's amazing how fast time goes when you're a parent. This week my oldest will turn 10, and I can still remember the day I brought him home from the hospital. It was November. It was the time of year when it's supposed to be beautiful and cold. Except we live in Texas, where it's summer practically year-round. So what it really amounted to was that I brought my son home with ankles the size of my knees, because the humidity made retaining water amazingly easy for a new mom. Thanks, humidity!

I remember that we would lay him in a bassinet right beside our bed, so that he could wake us up when he needed to eat. So that I could wake up at odd times and make sure he was still breathing. So that I could better convince myself that he was real.

He would sleep through his feeding time while I marveled at how he could do this. One of the mysteries of babies—they eat in their sleep. I didn't bring him into my bed, because he was so tiny, and in my worst-case-scenario mind, I actually saw myself rolling over and smothering him. So I would always gently lay him back in the bassinet where he would be safe until he stirred for the next feeding time.

He is turning 10 now. His head nearly reaches my shoulders—and I'm a tall woman. His legs are more than half of his body, spindly and slightly awkward. His hands are long and thin, without the bit of baby fat that makes them mushy. His eyebrows are thick and arched, and there is no hint of the puffy skin that I used to kiss when he was a baby.

It's amazing how quickly it's happened.

I think about this quick passage of time every time I pack up the clothes that my youngest has outgrown. It's the last time we will see these clothes. It's the last time we will see this stage.

This boy, though, is my first. He has been the first smile, the first walking baby, the first pre-teen with an attitude. He is the first boy who lit up when we bought him a LEGO set. He is the first boy who got to play Minecraft. He is the first boy who reached double digits.

I don't write about him much anymore, because he's getting to that age where he says he'd probably be embarrassed if any of his friends' parents were to read what I wrote about him. But because of this birthday, I have to write about him. Because all this time, he has held my heart.

The day we brought him home from the hospital, he held my heart in tiny little hands that would wrap around my first finger, just barely. Now he holds my heart in hands that fit just right, threading his fingers through mine.

He holds my heart in his hands when he calls me the worst mother ever. He holds my heart in his hands when he cries because he had a fight with his friend at school today, and he's not sure he'll have a friend tomorrow. He holds my heart in his hands when he is lying in bed, talking about how he just wants to give up.

He holds my heart in his hands when he tells me, without my saying it first, that he loves me. He holds my heart in his hands when he picks a flower he found on his walk home and he hands it to me, saying, "Put it in your hair." He holds my heart when he trusts me with something big and important, a secret he has to tell.

On good days and bad days, he holds my heart in his hands.

It's the same with all my boys. They hold my heart in their hands:

When they're hurting and they actually tell me why.

When they're silly and they don't tell me why.

When they can't figure out a math problem on their homework sheet and they call themselves dumb because of it.

When they can figure out the answer to a science question without any extra help and they call themselves smart and competent.

When they think that they're not quite as good as their brother.

When they believe they're of great worth.

When they think I'm mad at them.

When they recognize, for a moment in time, how much I love them.

When they say they want to run away.

When they say they never, ever want to leave this house, not even when they're grown.

When they scowl at me.

When they smile at me.

When they complain about doing their after-dinner chores.

When they help out without being asked.

When they have to be put back to bed a thousand times on a Friday night.

When they actually get in bed and stay there.

When they don't want to do what I've asked them to do and they do it anyway.

When they tell someone that I'm the coolest mom ever.

When they turn around in the next hour and say I'm actually the worst mom ever.

When they beat themselves up for doing something wrong.

When they congratulate themselves for doing something amazing.

When they say the world's a terrible place.

When they say the world's a wonderful place.

When they feel misunderstood.

When they feel known.

When they look so tiny in a school with such large walls.

When they look so big in our home.

When they say they hate me.

When they say they love me.

When they interrupt me.

When they leave me to myself for a few minutes.

When they teach me how to be myself.

It's a sad and treacherous thing to watch a child grow. The world is scary. We don't want them to be hurt. We don't want them to know what dangers await. We don't want them to ever forget who they are. But time moves on and we must move with it. And their hands, which hold our hearts, will eventually let go, and they will move along to someone else. But they will not be able to let go completely, because a mother's heart is always held within the hands of her children. No matter where they go, no matter what they do, no matter who they choose to be today.

My heart will always be theirs.

Dear Son: Here's What I Hope For Your Future

We don't have much more time with you. You are already 10, and I'm wondering how in the world I'm going to teach you all you need to know in the remaining eight years we have with you under the roof of our home.

"I'll be driving soon," you told me the other day, and I don't want to think about the fact that you will be, before we even know it. The last ten years have passed in a flash, and I can expect that the next eight will go even faster. Life has a way of speeding up when it's busy and when it's fun, and oftentimes I wish I could slow it down, press pause for a moment in time so that I could look in your black coffee eyes and observe your long and gangly limbs and delight in the smile that turns up at one corner of your mouth when you catch me staring at you.

I hope that you have much success in your life. I hope that your daddy and I have done our part. I hope that in the wild and crazy madness of our life with six boys, you have learned, along the way, that you are treasured. And I hope many other mighty things for you:

1. I hope you will know you have been deeply loved. I hope that you will, in your darkest moments, remember this forever and unchanging love. Even on the days when we can't seem to say a kind word to one another and all we can manage is fighting and snapping and twisting and flinging, I hope you know we love you. Even when

it feels like all the arguing and negotiating and lawyer-like finding of loopholes is highly inconvenient, I hope you will feel loved. Even when we're not doing the best job as your parents, or being the kind of people we really want to be because life is hard and fast and doesn't always wait for us to take a deep breath, I hope you know we love you. I hope you know that it does not matter who you choose to be today or tomorrow or six years into the future, you are always and entirely loved. I hope you know that you do not have to be perfect—you do not even have to be anywhere close to perfect, because we love you as much as we possibly could already. I hope you know you don't have to make all the best grades or achieve all the greatest achievements or make all the best choices, because we will love you regardless.

2. I hope you will know how very proud we are of you. You don't even have to do a thing. We will be proud of you no matter what you decide to do or who you decide to be. We will be proud of you for being alive, proud of you for choosing to be a good brother, proud of you for just existing in our lives and making it more vibrant and beautiful and wonderful. We were proud of you the moment you slipped into the world, and you didn't have to do a single thing to earn it. You don't have to do a single thing now to keep it, either.

3. I hope you will know that you will always have a safe place to fall. If you get out into the world and you discover that it's not a very kind place—if you don't happen to discover that while you're under the roof of our home—I hope you will see your daddy and me as a safe place to land. I hope you know that we're always on your side, that we're always in your corner. I hope you will know that you can trust us with anything that might be damaging or challenging your

heart. I hope you know that we always have your best interests in mind. I hope you know that we will always lift you back up to your marvelous self. We will be your net. We will sing your song when you forget it.

4. I hope you know that you will always have help back up—no strings attached—because this is what parents do. When you've gotten too down about your life and you can't seem to find a way out of the darkness, we will always be here to lift you to your feet again. I hope you know that you do not have to suffer alone, that you will always have a family on your side and walking with you through the hard and tumultuous journey of life. I hope you will know that our hands will always be stretched toward you, that we will be here, waiting, for your cry for help. We will walk you through enemy grounds, covering for you, and we will steer you in the direction you want to go anytime you've lost your way.

5. I hope you know that you do not have to try to be perfect. You can be imperfect because we are imperfect. I hope we have shown you our imperfections. I hope we have proven to you in our apologies and in our mistakes and in the things we have chosen to do and then changed our minds about. I hope we have shown you that you can fail and recover. I hope you will not expect perfection from the world or from yourself so that you will be free to love and create and be.

6. I hope that you know we are your biggest fans. There is no one who will yell louder for your success than we will. There is no one who believes in your success more than we do.

7. I hope you know the world is a wonderful one. I know sometimes it doesn't feel like it, but it is. We only have to open our

eyes to see the wonderfulness of the world. I hope you walk through it, always, with wide open eyes, ready to see. I hope you gather the light and let it drown out the dark.

8. I hope you learn that love is the whole and more than all. This is our family mission statement, and it describes everything about who we are. We want to be love and we want to walk in love. We want to infuse the world with love. I hope you love well and often and that you love everyone with whom you come in contact—however difficult that is or they are.

9. I hope you know that you can survive, that you are capable of great and mighty things. You'll have your ups and downs in life. You'll have to go through hard times. But what better way to learn what you need to learn than to endure those hard times and come out on the other side realizing that you're a survivor? You'll make it through whatever life throws your way, because every time you find light in the darkness, it becomes easier. I hope you always have hope.

10. I hope you know that you can do hard things. We've tried to teach you this, and this is why we make you do your homework on your own, as long as you can. This is why we let you do those intricate stop motion videos. This is why we encourage the healthy expression of your anger, because we want you to know that you can do hard things. You can conquer your anger. You can do that stop motion animation, even if the camera isn't working the way you think it should. You can do anything you set your mind to, even when it means tying your own shoes (remember how long it took you to do this on your own because you didn't really want to? And then how easy it felt once you learned how?).

11. I hope you know that we belong to one another. I hope you

know that all the world's people belong to you and you belong to them. This means that we should treat each other as a family. Some people won't do it, because not all are taught like you are, but you have to get used to treating them kindly anyway. Some people you just have to excuse from the normal rules of humanity, because no one taught them how to relate to other people. I hope you'll do that brave work. I hope you'll win their hearts through kindness.

12. I hope you know that love, joy, sadness, hope, anger, trust, heartbreak, and all the multitude of human emotions are acceptable. I hope you learn to feel passionately and wildly. I hope you can shape your passion in the right direction. I hope you experience the array of human emotions and their intensity—because this is how you learn how to be human. I hope you know gratitude and contentment. I hope you will trade in computers and phones for face-to-face meetings with people so you can look in their eyes and experience their emotions as well.

13. I hope you will be grateful for the small things, like a ball that is found in the early morning hours and the weather that is perfect for a day of playing dodge ball and the birthday party that maybe didn't have everything you wanted but included family you haven't seen in way too long.

14. I hope you'll learn how to play. I know it comes naturally now, and it's hard to imagine a time when it won't, but there will be a time. And I hope you retain this knowledge of how to play. It's easy for life to crowd out the importance of play, but I don't want you ever to lose it, because this is the way we remain alive and hopeful. Playing opens the door to creativity, which opens the door to a deeper and happier living. I hope you will always play, no matter

what you choose as your profession. I hope your job is your play.

15. I hope you will know and understand when to quit and when to keep going. I hope you will always know the difference between what you can change and what you can't change, and I hope you don't waste any time in trying to change yourself to be someone else's measure of success or perfection. I hope you will always be able to tell what works for you and what doesn't so you don't waste your time being someone else's definition of an acceptable man, employee, human. I hope you will always pursue knowledge and wisdom and continue growing but that you will know when something isn't going to work, no matter how much work you put into it. There is no shame in quitting if you're quitting for the right reasons.

16. I hope you know that you can be anything you want to be with the right amount of intentional practice. I say anything, but you're going to have to work really hard to overcome certain tendencies. That's not to say that this becoming will be easy. It's not. In fact, there are many adults who still struggle with it. And there's no shame in changing what you want to be, but I hope that you know whatever you choose, you'll have to do hard work and much intentional practice to become truly excellent at it. There's no one who is born with the talent to do anything they choose. There is always work that must be done in the arena of talent.

I know you don't have much longer in our house, and I want to make sure you know all of these things. But mostly I want you to know that we love you, no matter what, always. You are our pride and joy, and you will do spectacular things in this world. I have no doubt.

And I'm so glad I get to be your mother and watch it all unfold. I love you all the way to every solar system—discovered and undiscovered—and all the way back.

The Sentimentality Hidden in Baby Clothes

This week, I packed up my youngest boy's baby clothes. For good.

I cried, of course. They grow so fast when they're infants. Every time I reach for a new stage of clothes, I don't feel like I'm ready. I'm ready for the growing up, but I'm not ready at all. Not even close.

This last one has been different all along. He is the last baby who will wear these clothes that have passed down through all of his brothers. When he is done with them, they will leave their spot in our garage, where they have been pulled out, worn, and then repacked for the last eight years.

They will be given away. For good.

I am not a hoarder. I hate clutter like I hate spiders—freakishly—but this is one area where I struggle. Those tiny little clothes—were they really this small? I remember everything about them. I remember the outfit the firstborn was wearing the first time his giggle lit the night on fire with magic. I remember the shirt the second son had on the first time he smiled at me. I remember the jacket the third son had on when he came walking out of his brother's room on two feet instead of all fours.

I didn't expect clothes to hold within their fibers the fibers of our lives. My heart aches as I fold them away.

There are other reasons my heart aches.

I will never again lock eyes with a newborn in the labor and delivery room and feel the immediate love or the one that unfolds over days and weeks and months.

I will never again feed a baby in the gentle glow of a lamp during the earliest morning hours, when silence shimmers around us for once.

I will never again lie down with a newborn for a mid-afternoon nap—just because.

I will never again give a newborn a sponge bath on a bathroom towel because I am too afraid of water to dunk him in the bath.

I will never again hold that tiny weight in my arms and know that he is mine to kiss and snuggle and love for the rest of his days.

I will never again hear those sleeping grunts that tell me he's dreaming.

I will never again witness his laughter in sleep, when something wonderful I can't see flits across his dreamscape.

I will never again celebrate one of my babies rolling over on his own.

I will never again tell brothers to be careful with their baby.

I will never again fight through breastfeeding and feel guilty for giving up.

I will never again wake every few hours to feed a baby and celebrate over a stretch of four hours' sleep.

I will never again wait for a first smile or a first laugh or a first time he finds his voice.

I will never again be waiting with open arms to catch one of my children at the end of a first-walk.

I will never again celebrate a first birthday with a son or a daughter.

I will never again rock a child of mine to sleep because my smell is comforting and he is content.

I will never again watch a baby face fold into a smile when I reach to lift him from his crib in the mornings.

I will never again feed a baby cereal and try to dodge the sneeze that will spray it all over my face.

I will never again carry a burp rag across my shoulder, to catch the unexpected.

I will never again search the dryer for that missing infant sock I know I put in there half an hour ago.

I will never again use those floor blankets I made out of recycled T-shirts so he has a pretty place to rest his head when he's too tired.

I will never again read a story to a baby who doesn't understand words but only listens for the sound of my voice.

I will never again lift my baby to my shoulder and watch his face turn toward me because he wants to look in my eyes, and he'll do anything he can to make it happen.

I will never again dress him in clothes this tiny.

There is a pain in all of this. Transitions aren't easy with any babies, but they're especially hard with the last baby. There is a grieving, a heaving sorrow that comes with knowing that this is the last time, and it will be over in the blink of an eye. Most days I'm not ready.

But ready or not, the time has come.

So I put those clothes in the box, one of them held back—the one he was wearing the first time he smiled—so I can remember how small he was once upon a time. And then I close the box and write "Donations" on the side. Husband watches me. I nod.

He loads it into the car, kisses me, and drives off to deliver the clothes to another family who will use them. And that's when the water comes falling from a deep, wide hole in my heart.

That's when I cry.

The Paradox of 'Grow Up' and 'Stay Little'

It's bittersweet watching my boys grow. Some days I want them to grow up—past this 3-year-old argue-about-everything stage—and some days I want them to stay the little boy and little babies they are and were. Sometimes I'm thankful that they're clinging to my leg and whining, because they've gotten so big so fast, and other days I can't stand that they're clinging to my leg because I just want to have five minutes alone, to myself, without anyone telling me the color of their poop.

I am often reminded, in the course of even a day, how quickly they grow up. I remember how fast this time passes when they are climbing all over me and telling me they love me while their bony behinds are bruising my thighs. I remember how fast it passes when they bring me a flower and tell me that it's beautiful like me, and I realize it's been a while since I've had a wildflower bouquet. I remember how fast this time passes when we're late on our walk to school, and they can't be persuaded to leave the dandelions alone but must pick every one of them and blow their wishes to the sky—I know it won't be long that dandelions bring them such joy.

And then there are times when I'm eager for the season to pass: like the threenager stage or the potty-training stage or the won't-stay-in-bed stage, when I often, in my unguarded moments, think, *It will be so much easier when they're older.*

Back and forth I sway between wanting them to stay little and wanting them to grow up.

I want them to stay little when they're sitting on my lap and they tuck their heads into that special place right between my neck and my collarbone.

I want them to grow up when they're arguing with me over whether the sun is a broken off piece of the moon or it's the other way around, and, after five minutes of the argument, I just want to scream, "What does it even matter?"

I want them to stay little when they're saying how much they love me or showing me with slobbery, poorly aimed kisses.

I want them to grow up when they're screaming that they hate me because all their friends' parents let them play video games all the time, instead of limiting it to thirty minutes a day.

I want them to stay little when they're saying something that is so devastatingly cute that I just can't handle it.

I want them to grow up when they're speaking like they know everything about the world they could possibly know—way more than I know, and they're not open to argument. Or truth.

I want them to stay little when they bring me a book they want to read me, and they turn all the pages and act like they know the words that are written on them, even though they don't have all the language for this just yet.

I want them to grow up when they're getting into something I've told them a billion times not to get into—because surely when they grow up a little they'll be mature enough to follow instructions and rules.

I want them to stay little when there are little girls who come knocking on the door, asking if one of them is home, to which I reply, "No," even if he is.

I want them to grow up when they're asking me for a million things all at once.

I want them to stay little when they draw a picture of a spiky monster and call it their friend "Slimeball" and then address that picture to "the best mama in the world."

I want them to grow up when they're throwing pencils in my general direction because it's time to put the art supplies away and set the table for dinner.

I want them to stay little when we order pizza for dinner and they call us the nicest parents in the world just because of a food choice.

I want them to grow up when they're getting into the refrigerator for the thousandth time this hour because they're hungry and don't understand the concepts of "one snack a day" or "bored eating."

I want them to stay little when they're watching a presentation at the local museum and one of them drapes an arm around the shoulders of the other.

I want them to grow up when they're engaged in a slap-fight over who first looked at the jump rope and therefore gets to use it first.

I want them to stay little when they've just gotten ready for school and didn't need any extra help at all, leaving me a good fifteen minutes with nothing to do.

I want them to grow up when one is having trouble tying his shoes and another can't find his shoes and another is complaining about the current state of his shoes—which is nearly always ratty, except on the first day they're bought.

I want them to stay little when they thank me genuinely for pouring their milk, even though they can do it themselves.

I want them to grow up when they spill their milk for the third time in one morning and then complain about having to clean it up.

I want them to stay little when we sit around our dinner table playing the word game or making up stories together.

I want them to grow up when I'm already annoyed about the noise at the dinner table and they're laughing hysterically about the fart that someone just squeezed out.

I want them to stay little when they bring all their stuffed animals down into the living room, arrange them in a circle, and then plop down in the middle of it.

I want them to grow up when they refuse to take all those stuffed animals back upstairs.

I want them to stay little when they bring me a hurt that needs kissing.

I want them to grow up when that hurt that needs kissing is on their hind end and they blast hot air into my face when I brave the risk and kiss it.

I want them to stay little when they're talking to me about a story they really want to write and who the main character will be and how he will get out of his predicament.

I want them to grow up when they regard technology time as the best time of the day.

I want them to stay little when they say something in the growing-up voice that makes my chest ache.

I want them to grow up when they say something with a liberal dose of whine.

I want them to stay little when I watch them from across the room and imagine them as the baby and toddler they were.

I want them to grow up when I watch them from across the room and imagine the remarkable young men they will be.

Parenting is full of all kinds of paradoxes. This is just one of the many. There will always be days and moments when we can't wait for them to grow up, followed by moments when we long to freeze time and keep it here for a bit. Time always marches on. The best we can do is to enjoy those wish-they-would-grow-up moments right alongside the wish-they'd-stay-little-forever ones.

Store them all in the confines of our hearts and minds.

Kids Doing Chores: Is it Worth It?

Husband and I like to teach our children autonomy so that they can handle doing chores on their own, and, mostly, so that we can have a break from the array of chores plaguing us: washing the dishes, cleaning the bathrooms, taking out the trash, sweeping the floors, mowing the lawn, wiping the table and counters, dusting. All of these chores will be delegated, eventually, and Husband and I will live like the king and queen we are.

But first we have to pay a price.

The problem with autonomy—which children love, by the way—is that before you can actually achieve real and complete autonomy, you have to go through this time period I like to call "Pleasant Practice." The adjective there is sarcastic.

Here's what autonomy looks like during Pleasant Practice:

The 4-year-old, who is tasked with wiping the table, will wipe all the crumbs onto the floor, which the 6-year-old is trying to sweep, so the 6-year-old complains the entire time about how he just swept there and can we please make his brother stop wiping food onto the floor, because he's already asked and his brother keeps doing it and it's making it really difficult to finish sweeping the floor; he's going to be doing his chore forever and ever!

Another 4-year-old, who is tasked with washing the dishes, will pretend he's washing them but really is just using this "do the dishes" time as an opportunity to get off the bench where he sits for dinner and swing around sharp knives that, to be clear, Mama already had in their proper place inside the dishwasher but that he just had to take out because they're "in the wrong place."

The 9-year-old can be found usually pretending he is sick, especially if he is tasked with sweeping the floors this week. No one likes sweeping the floors, but he likes it the absolute least. In three weeks of being tasked with doing it, he's evaded it twenty times. And that means that he's been paying us to do it with his own hard-earned money—because a rule in our house is that if you want to skip your chores, you can pay someone to do it for you. I now have twenty dollars I didn't have before, which means I might be able to go buy myself a right shoe.

The 7-year-old will complain that he always has to do the trash and why does no one else ever have to do the trash, and can he please have a break because his birthday was five months ago and we forgot to give him a day off his chores (no, we didn't.). Which means all his other brothers will remind us about their birthdays and how we didn't give them a day off, either (we did.).

The 6-year-old will then be found smacking the wiping-the-table 4-year-old with the back of the broom, because every time he runs the broom across a square on the floor, another heap of mashed up carrots comes crashing down onto the floor again, because, apparently, the 4-year-old has not quite grasped the Brush It Into Your Hand technique his daddy went over in excruciating detail before handing the sponge back to him. What he's really doing is trying to wipe off the table as fast as he can so he can be free to terrorize the bathroom, which he will most definitely do when Mama's trying to wrestle a butcher knife out of the hands of his twin brother. Perfect opportunity provided in this Pleasant Practice.

The 9-year-old, who is this week assigned to wiping down the counters and cabinets, has, by this time, decided to join the fun. He sprays cleaner all over the counters, and no amount of sopping up and wringing out the sponge will soak up that pool. We have to bring in the help of beach towels.

Here's what we have at the end of Pleasant Practice:

The trash is accidentally dumped out because the one on trash duty tried to pull the bag out of the can and then set it on the floor to tie it, but before he could actually tie it, gravity took hold of it and toppled it on its side. Now there's a lot of whining and complaining about picking up all that trash on the floor. I can't help it. Trash is gross. And when all that's done, there's a gaping hole in the bag, because Trash Man drags it, instead of carrying it, out to the curb. At least he can find his way home again.

There are significant places that have been missed in the sweeping of the floor, including under the table. Sweeper Man says his arms aren't long enough to get under the table, and, besides, he thought he'd leave a little to feed the ants.

Plates and bowls and cups look haphazardly arranged in the dishwasher, in no particular order or place.

My hand sticks to the table when I foolishly test its cleanliness.

The counters are still sopping.

By the time chores are over, Husband and I will often ask each other, "Why do we do this again?" But the answer is simple. We have this fight and undergo this challenge every day because what chores do for kids is they show them they are part of a team, that they are expected to contribute to the current of our family life, and that they can do hard things with enough practice.

Not to mention these are life skills. They need to know how to wash dishes and wipe tables and sweep the floor. That means we have to take the time to teach them and let them practice in their own way.

And, eventually, our role in Pleasant Practice will no longer be needed, and we will, instead, be watching while they clean the kitchen after dinner.

At least that's what I tell myself when I'm trying to mop up some old mildewed strawberries from the floor because they took out another trash bag and it ripped in their still-novice hands and now I'm left with an even bigger mess to clean up.

One day I'm sure I'll be glad.

What Home Will Be Without Them: Incomplete

Husband takes the oldest boys to school and then packs up the rest to do a few errands, and I walk downstairs to breathe a little, refill my water, get a bite to eat. I round the corner and stop in my tracks. Every light downstairs has been left on, even though no one is home but me.

I shake my head, walk from room to room, flicking them all off, and while I'm tending to this walk-behind duty, I see pajamas left on the floor, shoes scattered about, food and plates left on the table.

And just when I'm feeling my annoyance the most, bemoaning the fact that I am the only one in my house who cares about an orderly house, a thought hits me right straight in my heart: One day they will be gone.

One day I will walk through a house that has remained still and quiet for hours, because one day they will be gone.

One day the floors will not look like a collection of dirty pajamas just multiplied while we weren't looking, because one day they will be gone.

One day I will walk in the front door, after an hour or two of running errands without them, and there will be no boy barreling into my legs or chest or belly, nearly knocking me from my feet, because one day they will be gone.

One day there will be no sticky-milk spots on the floor that will steal my socks or my slippers, because one day they will be gone.

One day there will be no more late-night knocks on our bedroom door, even though we've put them to bed twenty times already, because one day they will be gone.

One day there will be no couches squealing or moaning under the weight of somersaulting boys, because one day they will be gone.

One day there won't be eight plates to wash and eight forks to rinse and not enough leftovers for tomorrow's lunch, like we'd planned, because one day they will be gone.

One day we won't sit beside them while they take half an hour to read an easy reader book, because one day they will be gone.

One day we won't fight about the best time to do homework, because one day they will be gone.

One day we won't sign a billion papers and pack sack lunches they'll complain about later and help look for that missing library book, because one day they will be gone.

One day we won't have to pick up wet towels from the bathroom floor and wonder how no one seems to notice the towel racks waiting, because one day they will be gone.

One day we will walk past a bathroom and not think it smells like a swamp, because one day they will be gone.

One day we will do only two loads of laundry every week—light and dark—instead of the typical eight, because one day they will be gone.

One day we will walk by their rooms and there will be no LEGO piece explosions carpeting the floor, because one day they will be gone.

One day we will make our bed and it will stay made, because boys won't wiggle underneath the covers five minutes after we make it—because one day they will be gone.

One day the milk in the fridge will live past its expiration date, and so will the eggs and the carrots and the twenty pounds of fruit, because one day they will be gone.

One day we will rest our elbows on the counter and our shirt sleeves will not stick to the jam boys spilled while dressing up their toast a little, because one day they will be gone.

One day there will be no bath time or story time or silent reading time, because one day they will be gone.

One day the house will not shake with the shouts of boys and all the holes in the walls will be fixed for good and the houseplants will lift their heads again, as if to say, "Is it safe to come out now?" because one day they will be gone.

One day we won't throw another themed birthday party and brave all their friends helping destroy the house one party at a time, because one day they will be gone.

One day we will maintain perfect library records without fines, and we'll remember exactly where something is and we'll choose what movie to watch on a Friday night, because one day they will be gone.

One day we will turn on music without hearing, "Can we listen to KidzBop?" because one day they will be gone.

One day our game closet will stay closed and the card deck will stay a full deck and the puzzles will keep all their pieces, because one day they will be gone.

One day the floors won't be caked with mud tracked all through the house the day after it's rained six days straight and we sent them out to play, because one day they will be gone.

One day their bedrooms will smell like something besides dirty socks and wet dog, because one day they will be gone.

One day we will know just how much we enjoyed these days, because one day they will be gone.

Today, I walk around turning off lights, picking clothes up off the floor, wrinkling my nose at the smells slipping out of their bathroom even though the door is closed, and I think about what this place will be without them.

Tidy, orderly, quiet. Incomplete.

So I will enjoy them while I can.

That's Just...Weird

Things I Don't Understand About Boys

If you've ever wondered if aliens are real, all you have to do is be a mother in a household of boys.

Aliens are real, all right, and they're called boys.

When I was a kid, I played with Barbies. I sat quietly and read books without fidgeting and made my librarian mother proud. I knew how to take care of myself, and I enjoyed taking a bath.

Boys? No on every count.

When I look at my boys, I often wonder if I'm looking at an entirely different species—and, in fact, I am. The genders, as much as we may try to say that we're not all that different, are completely different. I know this because I live with seven males. My home is a controlled experiment. And maybe I'm more feminine than some women, but I believe that all my boys—Husband included—represent the spectrum of masculinity.

Just last night, I was wandering through my house, thinking about how I often wish it were a quiet house every now and then. I like my quiet, but my boys are hardly ever quiet. As I was wandering and wondering, my 9-year-old walked up to me with a giant booger on the end of his finger, stuck it in my face, and said, "Why do you think it has a black line down the middle of it?" and I gagged.

Some things I just don't understand about boys. Like the following:

1. Why they have to be so active all the time (and how it's even

possible).

They tire me out just looking at them. If it were up to me, I would call a time out and gladly sit on the couch reading for an hour or two. In fact, that's what I tried to do last Sunday afternoon, because we hadn't planned a Family Fun Day and I didn't really want to clean the house for the fiftieth time that weekend (that's how often the boys require it to be cleaned when they take out all the LEGO pieces and spread them over every surface in the house). I just wanted to relax for once. Problem is, I can't really relax because as soon as I stretch out on the couch, I am in danger of getting a bloody nose from the kid who's practicing his karate kicks in a flip over the side of the couch's arm. And I really don't want my cheek to meet that dirty foot, because I saw what's on the bottom of it.

2. Why they see a pile of laundry and think it would be perfect for messing up.

It never fails. I've just folded all the laundry and put it on the back of the couch, or on my bed, where it's slightly safer, and as soon as a boy sees it, those clothes no longer belong to anyone. They're in the community pile again, where they'll stay, because I'm not folding them again. Those clothes will remain strewn all over the place so when Husband comes home and asks me how my day went, he'll be able to take one look at the couch and know it must have been one of *those* days—he probably shouldn't even ask. It's like a secret message, created by clean clothes.

Every time my boys see a nicely stacked pile of anything, they'll play. Just this morning I was sweeping up some yard cuttings that Husband did yesterday because we got a homeowners association letter about one of our out-of-control shrubs (there are several), and my boys saw it and immediately walked right through the middle of it, because they thought it would be fun. Jobs are never done around these clowns.

3. Why they walk out of their shoes, promptly trip over those left-out shoes, and still don't get the message to put them away.

It's like my boys have a blind spot for shoes. Not only when they're removing them but when they're tasked with putting them on. Our house has a rule that shoes must go in one of two conveniently located shoe baskets, but this rule is rarely kept. Every time I walk in the house, I trip over shoes that are tossed haphazardly four inches from the shoe basket. Sometimes I only trip over one, because the other is clear across the room, probably sitting in the trash underneath an especially full volume of refuse, and nobody will notice until tomorrow morning, when they're frantically searching for shoes.

I've tried analyzing this phenomenon before, by the way. I've watched my boys walk right out of their shoes. Sometimes, if they're feeling particularly feisty, they'll walk out of one shoe and kick the other into the fan, where the shoe will skip, twist, and fly across the room for whatever target it can hit. They find great pleasure in this, no matter how many times we've told them not to do it. If you happen to see me with a black eye, believe me when I say it was a flying shoe.

This large blind spot when it comes to shoes also shows itself when it is time to leave and we are all running late and one of them, who shall remain anonymous for privacy reasons, bemoans the fact that he can never find his shoes.

"Did you put them where they go yesterday?" I say.

"Yes," he insists.

"Then why aren't they there?" I say.

"I don't know," he says, rolling around on the floor. I spot a shoe, pressed up against his hand. He picks it up and tosses it in the air.

"Is that your shoe, maybe?" I say.

"I don't see a shoe," he says.

"It's in your hand," I say.

It will take him five more minutes to realize that it is, in fact, a shoe in his hand and that the shoe is, miraculously, his.

Slightly worse than this is the kid who assumes that his shoes are out in the car. And then, once we get half an hour down the road, he remembers to tell us that his shoes were not actually where he thought they were.

"Did you bring me some shoes?" typically follows his admission, to which Husband and I do not even reply.

4. How they could possibly not be bothered in the slightest by that smell.

If you walk anywhere close to the passageway of my stairs or happen to actually climb those stairs, beware. The entire upstairs wing of my house smells like a swamp. This is mostly because the toilet in the boys' bathroom hardly ever gets flushed. They take "if it's yellow, let it mellow" quite literally. In fact, it doesn't even need to be yellow. It can be brown, too. No discrimination here.

Even if the offending toilet does happen to get flushed, the smell does not go away. It is held tightly in the walls, in the tile floors, on the ceramic counters. It is not going away anytime soon. But boys, fortunately, don't even notice it. Unfortunately, since I have to walk past this bathroom on my way into my bedroom every evening, I do notice it. I gag about fifty percent of the time. The other fifty percent, I happened to remember to plug my nose.

5. Their definition of quiet.

We have this nifty little time in our house that's affectionately referred to as "Quiet Time" for the older boys, nap time for the younger ones. Since my older boys are in school, we don't usually have to worry about whether or not Quiet Time remains a quiet time. But every month the boys have an early release day and every other week they have a day off from school, and then there are the weekends, of course, and summer. I'm always reminded during these six-kids-at-home days that a boy's definition of quiet is certainly not mine.

I will tell them thirty times in as many minutes that their brothers are sleeping, it's time to be quiet, but their volumes do not change at all. They can be reading books to themselves, and they are still loud. They can be drawing on separate sides of the room, and they are still loud. They can be writing a story in a journal and they are still loud (usually this is because they've written a story about a boy who gets around not by walking but by farting. You'd be amazed how many stories a boy can write about this fantasy.).

The purpose of Quiet Time, of course, is to give parents a break. We can snuggle in our room or work on something pressing or actually have a decent conversation at the table without boys interrupting. This is just a fantasy, however, so after a while, Husband and I give up on the quiet thing. We revise Quiet Time to Not Too Loud Time and resolve to do better tomorrow.

6. Their obsession with their unmentionables.

Nuts and berries, the goods, my private parts, whatever you

want to call them. Our boys have known from an early age that their penis is a penis and their testicles are testicles. We believe in teaching them the proper anatomical terminology. We also believe in teaching them modesty, but when it comes to the unmentionables, boys have a secret mission to sneak them into conversation, or find new ways to use them.

"Please put that thing away," is a typical admonition at my dinner table, mostly to the little ones. "Please don't talk about that" is another popular phrase, this one aimed mostly at the older boys. It doesn't matter how many times we say it. The words will be needed again. And again. And again.

7. Their preoccupation with all things that have a screen (except windows).

The only truly quiet time I get in my house is when my boys are sitting in front of some kind of screen. This is because it is the only thing in our house that can command their full attention. It's bliss, for the short time we allow. I wish I were the type of parent who would let them sit in front of screens all day and all night, but I'm not, so I only get 30 minutes of bliss every day.

But I do get the added bliss of a combined total of about seven hours when my boys talk to me about screens—the movie Husband let them watch today, the game they played with their friend, and, my favorite, Minecraft.

8. Their general and pervasive untidiness.

I like to think that I was pretty tidy as a kid. I mean, when my mother told me to put my clothes away, I at least stuffed them in a drawer, where they couldn't be seen. And when she told me not to leave my backpack on the table, I moved it to the floor instead, out of the way where it wouldn't bother anyone. When she told me to get my books off the couch where she'd like to sit, I just stacked them on the table beside the couch. Neat. Tidy. Contained.

My boys, however, leave their things everywhere. They have special hooks for their backpacks at the top of our stairs, but I will trip over those backpacks on my way down the stairs and nearly break my neck. They have a place for shoes, as I've said elsewhere. There is a place, in fact, for everything in our house. But boys will find a way to avoid those places—with gusto.

I'm always cleaning up after them, because I'm the only one who really cares about a clean and tidy house. I guess it's just payback for how much my mother cleaned up after me when I was a kid.

9. Their disinterest in anything remotely matching.

It's not unusual that my first-grader will come down the stairs with a blue and white horizontally-striped shirt and some blue plaid shorts. He doesn't care. Another son will wear brown shorts with black soccer socks pulled up to his ankles. He'll top the outfit off with a polka-dotted tie. My oldest son will wear his little brother's sweat pants, because he couldn't find any of his own, and even his teacher will notice and ask him if he picked up the wrong pants. It's hard not to notice when a kid's wearing pants that show not only his ankles but half his calves. And I haven't even breached the subject of shoes, which could fill an essay of its own. My boys don't believe in pairs of shoes. They believe in one shoe per foot, and that's the only requirement.

I know one of these days they'll care a whole lot about how they look, and then I'll long for the days when they didn't.

When I consider all of these differences between me and my

boys, I tend to think that men and women come from two completely different planets. Just as they are foreign to me, I am likely foreign to them. We are different in habits, in priorities, in the ways our minds and hearts unfold over the years.

But I sure am glad we ended up on the same planet, because I can't imagine life without these little martians rearranging my world.

The Disastrous 'Where Do Babies Come From' Talk

I knew the question would come. It always comes. Kids are curious beings, and they want to know about everything—especially babies.

We have what's called an "I Wonder Wall" that hangs in our kitchen. Our boys occasionally write questions on scrap pieces of paper and hang them on this wall. We take turns answering these questions around our dinner table in the evenings.

A question that has been hanging there for quite some time is this one: How do babies get in their mama's belly?

We've been avoiding answering this question for obvious reasons.

When I was a kid, the only sex education I got was in the fifth grade, when the teachers at my school sat us down and showed us a video. I remained naive about everything but sperm and eggs and periods and didn't really have any burning curiosity about where those sperm and eggs came from or how they worked toward fertilization.

And because I never had a conversation with my mother, I have no idea how to do this in the first place. I've jokingly told Husband that since we have six boys, this sex education will fall to him, but I also know that curious boys will ask their mothers questions.

And the second son did not disappoint. He asked questions the very day his last baby brother came home from the hospital. It's a mystery how a baby is in a mama's belly for nine months and then suddenly becomes not a large belly but a tiny human being.

That conversation—how the baby gets out—went about as well as can be expected.

I told him that women have this thing called a vaginal canal, and that's where babies sometimes come out, if they don't need to be cut out of their mama's belly. Well, why would they need to be cut? he said. Sometimes babies are too large to come out of a vaginal canal, I said. And where is the vaginal canal? he said. I pointed. His eyes got very large and he did not ask any more questions.

I knew they'd come later, and they certainly did.

One day, this same son came up to me with a confused expression on his face. "What was that canal you told me about?" he said. "A factional canal?"

"A vaginal canal," I corrected.

"What is it, exactly?" he said.

"It's where babies come out of their mama's belly," I said. "Like I told you."

"And where is it again?" he said.

I pointed.

"So you don't have a penis," he said.

"No," I said.

"Can I see it?" he said.

"Nope," I said. "You will just have to use your imagination."

Which is probably slightly worse, now that I think about it.

I powered on. "Anyway," I said. "A baby slides out of a vaginal canal and into the world."

"So we all came out that way?" he said.

"Yes," I said.

"What did Daddy do?" he said.

"What do you mean?" I said.

"What did Daddy do to help us be born?" he said.

"Well, he held my hand," I said. I didn't say that Husband also laughed hysterically at "Funniest Home Videos" while I felt like I was splitting in two.

"And how were we made?" my son said.

"With love," I said, evading the technical details. He was only 6, after all. I pointed to his question. "We have it on the I Wonder Wall. We'll answer it eventually."

"It's been up there for a really long time," he said. "So I thought maybe you could answer it now."

It was time to call in a reinforcement: Husband.

When Husband came into the kitchen, I said, "He wants to know how he and his brothers were made," and I absolved myself of the responsibility and let Husband take over the reins.

Now I know that, eventually, I can contribute something to this discussion, because I want to talk to them about things like valuing women and no meaning no and how a woman's body is not the property of a man, that women are much more than their bodies and the way they look, that they all need to be treated with kindness and respect. But this part of it? I feel pretty comfortable remaining on the outside. I don't need to know what Daddy and sons are talking about.

I didn't know until I was about 13 what actually happens during sex. And I found out when a friend came over and we walked down to a canal where my brother often fished and she laid it out for me.

She had older sisters, and her sisters had told her all about it. I didn't believe her. And when I asked my mom, she looked horrified that I would know something like this.

On the one hand, it is pretty daunting when you face a kid who knows nothing about sex and you have the responsibility of educating him or her about it. But learning from a parent, I think, is much better than learning from another kid who may not quite understand the nuances of intimacy and love. The best I can do, as the mother of boys, is to ask questions all the time. I want to root out what they know so that I can lay a better foundation for them.

I'm not quite ready to do that for a 6-year-old. My face got hot just thinking about it, because I'm an immature middle schooler when it comes to talking about sex. I have a little time to get over this. And I fully believe I will.

Husband, of course, bumbled through an explanation about seeds and flowers and blooming and my 6-year-old's head tilt got more and more pronounced. I'm pretty sure he was more confused than anything else when he finished that conversation with a, "Hmm," and then ran off to play on his scooter.

Husband and I looked at each other. "I really messed that one up, didn't I?" Husband said.

I patted him on the arm. "Well," I said. "He's only 6. I'm sure we'll get another few chances."

Later that night, I heard my 6-year-old explaining to his younger brother that they all started out as bean seeds, and then Mama drank some water and food, and they became babies.

I guess kids will frame what they need to know in whatever context they can to make it understandable. Which is just fine by me.

One day they'll want to know more. And I'll be prepared to tell them.

The Joy of Wearing a Birthday Suit

When I was a sophomore in college at Texas State University, I did a story on the college streaker. Every holiday, this guy would streak through the Quad and up to Old Main, where the journalism classes and the newspaper offices were. He would outrun all the campus police, though they mostly ignored him because it was all in good fun and had been a continuing tradition for at least twenty years. He was affectionately known as the Holiday Streaker. He would wear nothing but a prop, positioned in front of his goods.

I was terrified to do this interview. I didn't understand guys and their obsession with nakedness. But, thankfully, he was clothed while I conducted the interview.

Fast forward ten years, and now I'm the mother of six boys. I see nakedness—even the unwanted kind—every day. I never cease to be surprised by it.

What is it about boys and their nakedness? I don't really know. I do know, though, that every time I get ready to snap a really cute picture of one of my boys, there's usually always a penis in the way.

You hear a lot of boy parents talk about how their boys like to run off naked after a bath. It's true. It's like wrestling a herd of longhorns into a pen just trying to get boys to put on some underwear after a bath. They're wild and free, and they would like to remain so. Sometimes we won't even know they're still wild and free when they go to bed, because they've wrapped a blanket around them so efficiently that we have no idea what lies beneath. They'd sleep naked, emerge from the house naked, probably even go to school naked if we let them.

I can't fully comprehend this fascination with being naked, because the last thing in the world that I would want to do is walk anywhere naked.

It's not just after baths that my boys like to strip. They'll do it in the middle of the day, when there are hours of sunlight left before bedtime. They'll come in from playing out front with their friends, and even if it's the dead of winter and freezing cold in our house because we like to save energy by not running our heater, they will strip down to their birthday suits and start jumping all over the couch. They'll streak through the kitchen and upstairs to their room, and we better hope that all the curtains are closed so the neighbors don't get a show they didn't really want to see. We've boarded up most of our windows for this very reason. I'm just kidding. We've only boarded up the window in the twins' rooms, and that's just because we caught them hanging out of it one night when they figured out how to unlock it and punch out the screen.

It's gotten so bad in our house that we had to actually make up a rule that anyone who expected to be served dinner at our dinner table had to at least come clothed in underwear. This was mostly for the 4-year-old twins, who, for some reason, preferred eating naked to fully clothed, which didn't make any sense at all, because everybody knows when a 4-year-old eats spaghetti, the shirt is just a napkin. Instead, they would use their bellies for a napkin, which seems like it would be much less efficient. Not that I want them to wipe their hands on their shirts. It's just that sometimes I forget to wash the cloth napkins, and then we're all wiping our hands on our shirts. Well, except for Husband and me. Or maybe. You'll never know.

We also had to make a rule that if a boy wanted to sit on Husband's back during the night time story reading, which is after their baths, they had to be wearing underwear.

Despite these apparently innocuous rules, my boys have a hard time keeping their clothes on. They will take them off at the slightest provocation. One day one of the twins dropped a piece of popcorn on his shirt, and he stripped it off, saying he didn't want to wear a dirty shirt. A piece of popcorn. That hardly had any butter on it. But the way it grazed his shirt turned his shirt too dirty to wear.

Now that we're in the middle of a Texas summer, I can sort of maybe get it. When I go outside the house, I wish I was walking around naked, too. And I know, deep down, that it's perfectly normal to want to walk around naked, because it is, after all, how we come into the world. Other cultures don't find the naked body quite as offensive as the American culture does. But I do have to say that when you're a mom of only boys, and nakedness crops up every other minute, it does get slightly annoying. I would like to snap pictures of them every now and then, without a renegade penis framed in the shot. And I'm not interested in how much your penis has grown since yesterday, thank you.

Getting a boy dressed in the morning is like trying to hold down an angry alligator who wants to pull you down to the bottom of the swamp. And because my upstairs smells like a swamp, courtesy of the boys' bathroom, it's not hard for my imagination to believe that's really happening.

At times, I've even been shocked by an unexpected naked body. Here are a few of them:

When I'm walking out of the bathroom myself, and there's a boy who was fully clothed a second ago now sitting down playing the piano in nothing but his skin and a fedora hat.

When I'm cooking dinner and I turn around to see a naked boy streaking past me on his way out the back door. NOPE.

When I'm reading a book and someone jumps off the couch onto the floor, and I see he's no longer wearing the Spider-Man costume, and, also, he somehow lost his underwear.

When they were just sitting down to the dinner table fully clothed and I turn around to load a few dishes in the dishwasher, and they strip in record time for a naked game of chase around the living room.

When they're having a dance party and they get too sweaty and solve that terrible problem by stripping.

I really shouldn't be surprised by any of it anymore. But, for some reason, I always am. Nakedness never becomes less than shocking. Even when you're a mother of six boys.

Every now and again, the boys forget themselves and strip when it's inappropriate to strip. Or they do something else related to streaking that's inappropriate. Or they fight with us about why they should wear clothes. This means we've had to come up with some rules regarding stripping and an appropriate dress code for the home. Rules like:

1. If someone is over at our house for dinner or just to talk or to babysit, all clothes must remain on your body.

2. If you're really excited about the new Olaf underwear you just

got, you cannot simply pull off your pants in the middle of the grocery store so you can show your skivvies to the woman in line behind us being extra nice to you.

3. In fact, you probably shouldn't even talk about your underwear with strangers. Why? It's not polite conversation. I know you don't understand what polite is, judging by the smacking you do at the dinner table, but trust me. Polite will get you far in this world (mainly because you'll be a minority).

4. If you need to go potty while someone is visiting our house, you must be fully clothed before coming back out of the bathroom.

5. Underwear, at the very least, is required for sitting at the dinner table.

6. You must have underwear on to climb on Daddy's back after baths. Same goes for sitting in Mama's lap or lounging on any of the furniture anywhere in the house. People don't appreciate butt crack anywhere near them.

7. You must make sure your underwear does not remain on the floor of your room but makes it into the laundry basket so that Mama can wash it and you don't have to answer the question "Why are you naked?" with "I don't have any clean underwear." That is not a valid excuse anymore. Wear them inside out and then backwards if you have to. It'll teach you to get your skivvies where they go.

8. Wearing the same underwear for four days in a row is not allowed, even if they're your favorite pair. Unless you don't have any others clean. If that's the case, see rule number 7.

9. If you're going to play outside—even if it's 104 degrees in the middle of summer—you must be fully clothed.

10. No, you cannot jump on the trampoline in our backyard

while you're naked. Get in here right this minute and put on some clothes.

11. If you want to be in family pictures, you must be fully clothed. You don't want to be in family pictures? Too bad. Get dressed.

12. If you want me to take a video of you performing acrobatics on the couch, you must be fully clothed.

13. You should never stand on your head when you're naked and have to pee. Yes, it is possible to defecate on your head.

14. Hands don't belong in your underwear. Get them out. Get them out. GET THEM OUT OF YOUR UNDERWEAR.

15. No, girls don't have penises, and it's not okay to pull down Mama's workout pants just to make sure.

Who would have ever thought we'd have to make so many rules about the appropriate attire in our house and out in public? But a word from the wise: Boys will require a whole lot of I-didn't-think-I'd-need-to-make-this-rule amendments. This is only the beginning.

I know these rules will be revised over the years, because my oldest is only 8, and I live in a house with seven males. I don't even know all my boundaries yet.

But it's a good place to start.

(HEY! NO, YOU MAY NOT PLAY HIT-MY-BROTHER-IN-THE-PRIVATES. GET YOUR CLOTHES ON.)

Welp. Looks like we have a rule number 16.

How to Dress Like a Boy

I used to care a whole lot about the way my boys dressed. I would doll them up for family pictures and make sure their hair was just right or, if they'd slept on it wrong, I'd toss a really cute hat on top of the mess. I worked hard to make sure they had matching shoes—not just shoes of the same color and style but shoes that actually matched their outfits and complemented each other. I matched their socks and sometimes even their underwear.

No, I never went that far, because half the time my boys weren't wearing underwear in the first place.

When I look back at all these early family pictures, which depict our stylishness and prove that I was not always dressed in workout clothes, I miss them a little. Husband and I made it look like we actually had it together. I'd like to look like I have it together every now and then.

But then I think about how much time it takes to get boys to actually care about the way they look, and I think, nah, it's not worth the effort.

I have friends who are newer parents than Husband and me, because we started a little early, and these parents spike up their kids' hair and dress them all cute for every single circumstance you can imagine, and when I see those cute little boys dressed by their parents, I think to myself that they'll give it up in a few years, too. Eight years of parenting and all the battles and challenges that come with it have made me something akin to apathetic when it comes to what my kids wear. Now I'm just glad they walk out the door wearing matching shoes—and half the time one 4-year-old can't even manage that, which he'll point out to every teacher in the kindergarten hallway as we drop his older brother off at school.

This morning, on the way to school, this particular child, who is a twin, wore one flip flop and one tennis shoe—not because he couldn't find the matching shoes but because he wanted to. The 7-year-old wore shoes that his two biggest toes poked through, even though he has perfectly fine tennis shoes that don't have holes at all. When I pointed this out, because I didn't want his teacher to think that we're in such a bad state that we can't get him adequate shoes, he said he preferred these shoes, because they left a little breathing room for his feet. I said, fine, do whatever you want, but don't call me when the soles fall off.

It flapped all the way to school.

Occasionally I marvel at this strange person I have become. The person I used to be would never, ever have agreed to let her child, essentially a representation of herself, walk outside the house like that. Now I feel perfectly fine allowing a boy to walk out the door in a navy blue and cerulean striped shirt with bright green pants that have gaping holes in the knees, because there are much more important battles I will have to fight during the day. I don't care if a kid goes to school in two left shoes. I don't care if a kid woke up with Einstein hair that they didn't even try to comb. I don't care if they wear shorts on a 30-degree day. They are in charge of their own wardrobe.

Full disclosure, I do still make an effort for family pictures. We're paying for those things, and I don't want them to go down in history as proof that we were drowning beneath waters of our own making.

For the everyday, no family pictures dressing, my kids look like feral felines who thought they'd take a stab at wearing clothes. I try not to let it bother me. Every now and then I have to draw a line. My 5-year-old has this workout shirt that's a pretty blue color. It looks really good on him with his naturally tan skin, but he has worn it so often that now it looks like it's been dragged through a pile of mud even after I've scrubbed it with dish soap (which is my eco-friendly solution for stain remover) and washed it. There are stains on this shirt that will never come out. So when he puts it on, I always tell him to change. He can wear it around the house, but not to church or school.

The other day, Husband attempted a talk with the 9-year-old about the proper dress for church, because we've gotten a little lax about the appropriate attire now that we're working for one that requires extensive travel on Sunday mornings and we have to get up early.

Husband: From now on, you need to wear shoes to church, not flip flops.

9-year-old: Okay.

Husband: And also no sweat pants with holes in them.

9-year-old: Okay. And I should probably also wear underwear.

Well, yes, that would be nice.

But, you see, these are the kinds of things that I've stopped caring so much about. Because there are so many other things to care about. Like their hearts and how they feel about what happened at school today and whether there are any concerns that they have about friends or bullies. I don't have the time or energy to spend my days caring about what they look like when they walk out of the house. Soon enough, they'll all care about the way they look, and then we'll never find our way back to that innocent time of early childhood when they thought that sweat pants paired with a button-up shirt qualified as dressing up. And I don't think I'm quite ready to leave that time yet, because leaving it will be an arriving of sorts. They get to remain children as long as they don't care about what they look like, but as soon as they start caring what they look like, they become young men. I want to enjoy the childhood. So I've loosened my grip on this.

If they want to look like a fashion experiment gone wrong, so be it. After all, most days I look like I just finished at the gym. In fact, to most of the parents at my boys' school, I probably look like I do nothing else but spend time at the gym.

Well, except for the few extra pounds I carry around.

Things You'll Hear in a Household of Boys

If you listen closely enough, you'll hear a whole lot of interesting things in a household of boys. You might not even have to listen all that closely, because often you'll hear shrieks when they get into a fiery fist fight that's over before it even began. There's the squelching of a plunger when they decide this is a job they would love to do, even though they're only 3 and they haven't gotten parental permission. You'll hear talk about who had the biggest and grossest booger on their finger for the longest amount of time, because these are the types of competitions boys have.

And that's just from the boys. What you'll hear from the parents of those boys is equally interesting.

Here are some of the most frequent things you'll hear from parents in my house of boys:

1. "Put that thing away."

If you have never experienced the pleasure of eating with a boy, you will likely not know to what these words refer. Allow me to enlighten you. My boys—the little ones, not the big ones anymore—occasionally like to pull out their unmentionables and examine them while we're eating. They also like to emerge from the bath dripping wet and run naked in order to dry. In the middle of a Texas summer, they will strip down to their birthday suit as soon as they come inside the house, because it's so hot they can't even bear to wear clothes. And while I don't blame them for stripping down, because

I'd do it if I wasn't a woman, I would also like to go five minutes without seeing a flash of a naked boy streaking through the house. I would like to have a little moment to eat my food without having to tell them, for the twelfth time, to put that thing away.

2. "I'd prefer less potty humor."

It is so funny when someone farts or someone digs for gold and comes out with a large and gooey chunk of it or someone has some kind of joke about vomit or diarrhea or fart-triloquy that his brothers haven't yet heard. My boys will laugh for days at any of these things. And when is the best time to rise to the challenge of potty humor? That's right. Dinnertime.

At the table, while we're eating spaghetti, someone will sneeze, and a large glob of snot will shoot out of his nose onto his hand, and he will proudly hold it up for all to see. Also at the table, someone will fart for a whole minute, each motorboat pop shaking out in time with a boy's laugh, and the table will dissolve into giggles, at least until the sulfuric fumes reach noses and they all pass out instead. At the table, a boy will repeat the joke his friend told him about diarrhea and maggots.

No thanks.

We've had long and drawn out talks about what is appropriate dinner conversation. They've gotten slightly better, but every now and again, they forget the rules and what manners they actually retain. And then they'll talk the entire time about who has the grossest booger, who has the smelliest and loudest fart, and who executed the most rattling burp (this honor usually goes to Mama).

3. "You're not hungry, you're just bored."

In the summertime, this becomes a mantra in our house. On

grocery day, the boys will pillage the refrigerator until there's nothing left for the rest of the week, and then the cries grow ever more desperate.

"I'm sooooo hungry," they'll say when confronted with an empty refrigerator of their own making.

It doesn't matter that they just finished eating three pounds of blueberries, they're still going to be hungry. If they just wolfed down a whole loaf of bread with three sticks of butter, they'll tell me they're still starving. If they have gone more than five minutes without something to chew on, they'll be dying of hunger. We had to buy gum just to trick their stomachs into thinking their jaws were crushing nutritious food.

They eat about forty-three pieces a day.

4. "Do you know the definition of quiet?"

Boys cannot do anything at all without making noise. They walk up the carpeted stairs and it sounds like they have thousand-pound boots on their feet. They're sneaking into the kitchen to nab one of those cookies I made last night, and their breathing sounds like the scary blob monster that lived in my closet when I was a kid. They go to the bathroom at night, and the walls shake.

I'll never understand how they can possibly be so loud.

5. "Please stop fighting."

Summertime is the best time to hear this in practice. My boys fight every other minute. Sometimes they're fighting with words like, "That's not fair," and "I'm telling," and, "You better not!" But sometimes this fighting gets really entertaining, like when they're all gathered around Pokémon cards and their oldest brother makes a trade that the others don't agree with (because, as the oldest, he's more enterprising than they are), and they'll duke it out with a game of Hit Me In the Face, and whoever cries first loses. This is fun to them. I know. Crazy.

In a house of boys, you'll hear things like smacks, slaps, punches, and faces planting against the ground when someone is knocked over. There are also things like knuckle punches and head butts, which sound mostly like sickening thumps that will turn your stomach, and then other indescribable noises that will sometimes concern a mom until she turns around and the boys are laughing, not bleeding.

I've gotten really good at shaking my head in wonder.

6. "Go put on some clothes."

Anyone who has the privilege of raising a son knows that boys like to run around naked. It starts at birth. My baby enjoys getting out of the bath and streaking through the house, yelling, "Cute!" as in, "Look how cute I am." And he is. Super cute.

Unfortunately, 4-year-olds don't understand that they can't utilize this same freedom when guests come over to dinner or a babysitter shows up to free us for a couple of hours on a Friday night. They also don't understand that they can't go outside in their underwear. Or how it could possibly be cute for a 1-year-old to walk around in his birthday suit but it's no longer appropriate for them.

Growing up is hard, kids. Go put on some clothes.

7. "What's that smell?"

The answer to this oft-repeated question in our house is usually simply boy. Boys can be blamed on any smell. They are responsible for the reek coming from the upstairs bathroom. They are responsible for the wet-dog smell that permeates our library when it's story time and they've just come in from playing outside. They are responsible for the sulfur cloud hanging over our house, unless we've had broccoli for dinner, and then it's likely me.

8. "The toilet is overflowing."

I think our boys have broken our toilet. Every other day, one of the two toilets they're allowed to use (because I refuse to share the third one with them) clogs. I don't know if someone is just toilet-paper happy or if it's because no one can ever be bothered to flush, but in the case that someone does flush, these words are often heard just after the flushing sound. Most of the time the toilet is not actually overflowing, it's just clogged up because someone threw a whole roll of toilet paper—cardboard part and all—down the toilet to see what would happen. Thanks, twins. You always make life easy.

9. "You might want to go check your pants."

Boys are really proud of what comes out of their body, especially when it concerns stinky air from between their hiney flappers. My boys, when they feel an especially large fart bubble coming, will push it out proudly. Oftentimes, you can tell by the look on their face whether they've pushed slightly too hard. You can also tell by the wet sound. The perpetrator will often look momentarily bewildered and then a little concerned, after which one or both parents will say, "You might want to go check your pants."

And what you'll hear next could go either way.

10. "You're especially wild tonight."

The energy that boys contain is astounding. I get done with my day and the only thing I want to do is lie down in my bed and read for a little bit. This is how I relax. Apparently, when boys are tired and ready for bed, they recline the recliner, use the elevated foot rest as a diving board and try to make it to the couch without falling in the carpet lava.

Now. I love that they're imaginative. But I'm trying to relax. I don't want to hear the noises of boys tromping all over the place when I've spent a whole entire day hearing it.

It's not just bedtime, either. We have a long bedtime routine that's designed to ease boys into relaxation and slumber, starting with a nice and soothing bath. They'll get out of the bath and scare each other on their way out to the library for story time. They'll sit in the library for Silent Reading and will crack loud jokes to one another instead of reading silently like they're supposed to do. We tell them it's bedtime and they decide to sneak downstairs and do headstands on the floor while their feet are balancing 10-pound weights. Not only is it dangerous, but it's annoying.

11. "Get back in your room" or some other instruction that you have to repeat a thousand times.

My twins are especially bad at following instructions, particularly mine. Husband would blame this on the scientific evidence that men don't actually hear women all that well—science says that women's voices are too soothing and lure men into a state of rest rather than action. But you know what? I don't care. I expect kids to follow my instructions (or have a really good reason not to) when I open my mouth. My twins just act like they can't hear.

Because we spent a month of nights where my twins would wander while the household was sleeping, we installed a backwards lock on their door (Findings during their nightly wanderings: An empty tube of Toms strawberry toothpaste, toothbrushes shoved under their pillows, new permanent marker art on the doors, a plunger propped beside their bed, an empty bottle of children's vitamins, an empty vial of peace and calming essential oil—which didn't work, apparently. For a while there, Poison Control knew our names. And then we wised up and locked them inside for their own protection). So now I don't have to tell *them* to get back in their room anymore. But the older boys have not let me forget what the repeated instructions sound like. I have to tell them at least three times each night. I'll never understand this aversion to bedtime. I wish someone was telling me to go to bed at 8:15.

12. "What were you thinking?"

This is probably the most commonly repeated phrase in my house. And the answer is usually "Nothing." As in, they aren't thinking anything. They don't think about what could possibly happen if they decide to ride a skateboard down the stairs. They don't think about the consequences of trying to stand on their heads while their feet are balancing ten-pound weights. They don't think anything but, "That sounds like a lot of fun" when their brother dares them to step in an ant pile and stay there for a whole minute.

Even though sometimes I wish I had a sound board where I could push the right key so the pre-recorded words I always need to repeat plays for them over and over again and I don't have to waste time and breath, I can't imagine my life any other way but this one: wrapped around a whole tribe of boys.

It really is a beautiful life.

Things You'll Never Hear in a Household of Boys

I don't know what it's like to live with girls. Well, I take that back. I remember living with three girls in college, and I remember my mom joking with me about how the powers that be must have been preparing me for a life with a messy husband.

Little did I know that the powers that be were actually preparing me for life with *six boys* and a husband. Silly me. I didn't dream big enough.

Now. I know that girls can be just as messy as boys, but I also know that I am a neat and tidy person, for the most part. I imagine that, if I had a daughter, she would share my propensity toward neat and tidy—no way would I end up with THAT many messy kids.

All that aside, there are some other things I've noticed about my boys: they can be selfish little twerps. I know, I know, most young kids are. And I know we can teach them to be selfless and clean and tidy—and it's our duty, really, because it's clearly not the way they're born.

But there are also some things I imagine will never change in a household of smelly, wild boys.

Like the things they say—or don't say.

Here are some things you'll never hear in a household of boys:

1. "It's OK. You take the last taco, brother."

Feeding time at my house is quite an event. The most accurate description I can pull out of my writer brain is "Feeding frenzy."

With so many starving boys who haven't eaten in the last hour (when they consumed, impressively, a whole pound of carrots in one sitting) vying for space and a serving spoon, there's likely not to be anything left by the time I get around to the table—except for the asparagus no one likes because once the oldest got it stuck in his throat, and when he pulled it out, the string just kept coming, like a comic representation of a magician pulling a scarf from his throat.

Taco night is, by far, the worst.

Because the boys are still young (the oldest is only 8), they need help making the tacos (we'd likely run out of meat by the fourth taco —because they'll fill the shell to the top in an effort to shovel as much food into as little space as possible). But the problem is, by the time we've made the taco for Boy Number 5, because Boy Number 6 doesn't eat adult food yet, Boy Number One is already done with his taco and is (politely) asking for another. We usually make him wait until Husband and I have eaten our first taco, too, hoping that this rule will make him chew instead of inhale. Of course that never works.

But worst of all is when there's only one taco left. The boys all look at each other, daring a brother to reach for the shell so they can smack his arm right off his torso.

I will never, ever hear those gracious words, "No, you take the last taco."

Instead, we will slice it up into tiny little pieces and listen to the words that always follow this solution: "Aw, no fair! He got a bigger piece than me."

2. "Well, I didn't win. At least I had fun."

I have never heard a boy say this. I don't think any parent has ever heard a boy say this, because when you're a boy, you only want to win. It's not because your parents teach you that winning is everything (we sure didn't). It's just that this is part of who you are. Second place is for people who shouldn't be playing anyway.

About once a week, for Family Time, we'll break out the board games to play. I don't know why we do. We always go in thinking that this time will be fun, because they're a week older and they've got one more loss under their belt, and surely they'll realize that even though they lost last week they're still alive. The world didn't end, and, bonus, they're still happy, for the most part. And yet, inevitably, as one player's token nears the finish line before the others, my blood pressure begins to rise, along with a wedge of anxiety in my throat, because I know someone's about to melt down.

"Aw!" the loser says. "I wanted to win." And then he starts crying about how he never, ever, ever wins and he's just going to quit.

"It's not about winning," I'll say. "It's about having fun." He just looks at me like I'm an extraterrestrial with a rutabaga growing out of the top of my head—part amazement, part confusion, part disgust.

I'm still waiting for those words, but I fear they'll never come.

3. "It's completely fair that he gets to stay up later than I do."

This one works with many different phrases. "It's completely fair that he got the bigger strawberry." "It's completely fair that he had five friends come to his birthday party and I only had four." "It's completely fair that he gets to wear a black shirt."

There is nothing fair in the life of a boy.

I've tried explaining the difference between just and fair, but this is a lesson lost on my boys right now. They're still young. They see in mostly black and white, which means it's not fair that one brother gets the longer straw. It's not fair that one brother gets the superhero cup. It's not fair that one brother is using more air or weighs more or grew more inches in the last year.

It's hard for kids to see fair as it should be seen.

"It's not fair," the 6-year-old said yesterday morning.

"What's not fair?" I said.

"He gets a bowl of oatmeal," he said.

"You also got a bowl of oatmeal," I said.

He cocked his head. "Oh. Oh yeah," he said.

I shook my head and waited for the next declaration of "it's not fair" to come. And it did, three minutes later, when the 8-year-old showed up at the table wearing a pair of sweat pants and the 5-year-old thought it wasn't fair that his brother had clean sweat pants while he did not.

4. "Don't worry, Mama. Of course I know better than to try that."

I wish I could say I've heard these words or that I'm confident I will hear these words in the future. But in a household of boys, I don't think this is possible. I'm speaking purely from experience.

I didn't hear these words from the 8-year-old, who attempted to walk up the stairs in roller blades while I hobbled up in my broken-foot boot. I didn't hear them from the 6-year-old, who tried a headstand three stairs up and slid the rest of the way down on his face. Not from the 5-year-old, who wanted to see what his pee would look like if he peed off the top of the minivan out front. Not from one 3-year-old, who wanted to see what would happen if he tried to put two CDs into the CD player and push play. Not from the other

This Life with Boys

3-year-old, who thought he'd unstop the toilet paper mess in his favorite toilet with his brother's plastic yoda puppet (Fix it, I will).

Boys don't have these critical thinking skills down, and I hear it's a long time before they master them.

But you know what I do hear in a household of boys?

"I really, really, really love you, Mama."

And that's more than enough.

The Transformative Nature of Boys

A Crash Course on Living With a Man

I did not live with a man before I married Husband. It's true that I shared a house with messy roommates all during my college years, and I did my fair share of complaining about living with those messy females. (My mom would just laugh when I complained. I know it's because she thought I deserved those messy roommates because I hadn't exactly been a tidy teenager. I know this because when I think about my boys one day complaining about their own messy roommates—if they even notice, that is—I think I'll probably laugh with glee, too).

But those roommates were nothing compared to living with a man.

When Husband and I moved in together after our honeymoon days at Disney World, I was not prepared for all the ways we would do things differently. I guess it was good practice for raising six boys, but it sure was an awakening experience, to say the least.

He squeezed toothpaste from the bottom.

Maddening. Everyone knows that squeezing a toothpaste container from the top is what you're supposed to do, so when you're only left with a little bit in the tube, you can roll it up and feel much more satisfaction for getting something out of it and onto your toothbrush. If you're constantly squeezing the tube from the bottom and roll as you go, you don't have that same exquisite pleasure that there's still some left and you bought yourself another day. There's no surprise to it at all. Lame.

He didn't hang up his clothes after laundry day.

Before we had kids, Husband and I lived in tiny little apartments with closets that were about the size of our rooms. We thought we were so lucky to have those walk-in closets—until I realized what Husband was going to use them for. That's right. He used them for piling his clothes inside. Not hanging them up. Piling.

I couldn't walk in a walk-in closet for years without stepping on clean clothes. "I'll put them away tomorrow," he always said. Tomorrow came and went. I still walked on a clothes carpet.

Over the years this has evolved. It began in our closet, and then we finally had The Talk, because I had to use the closet, too, and I didn't like stepping over clothes all the time just to find something I could wear. I'm not the most graceful person in the world, and I was a runner. I didn't want to sprain my ankle on something as silly as a mountain of clothes and not be able to run for six weeks. So the piles moved to a wing chair in our bedroom. And then they moved to his side of the bed, which means that come bedtime, they move to his side of the floor.

He's the one tasked with helping the boys put away the laundry, since I do all the actual washing and folding, and all they really have to do is make sure they get their clothes in the dirty clothes hampers (which is apparently a really hard thing to do), but I'm starting to think that maybe this wasn't the wisest plan, since most of the time all that laundry gets stacked and left out on banisters instead. Mt. Clean Clothes has spawned.

He walked out of his shoes and left them there.

If I had a dollar for every time I got up to go to the bathroom in the middle of the night and tripped over one of his gigantic clodhoppers, we wouldn't have driven an old Honda Civic for the first five years of our marriage.

He left his plate in the sink without rinsing it off.

This wouldn't have been a huge deal. The problem was really that he liked to eat ranch dressing with everything. Have you ever smelled ranch dressing when it's been sitting on a plate for a few hours? Disgusting. I couldn't stand the smell, which perpetuated the problem, because once something got to where I couldn't stand the smell, I wouldn't rinse it off, either, which means the ranch dressing would make itself comfortable, hardening and inviting its moldy friends to come around and play.

Husband, of course, would turn a blind eye to the dishes with ranch dressing piling up in the sink, even though I'd done three loads in the dishwasher since the ranch had solidified. We used paper plates for a while after that, especially when I got pregnant with our first son and projectile vomited every time I came in contact with ranch dressing.

He put the detergent in after he started the washing machine.

Um. No. This little "master technique," which is what he called it, left all sorts of streaks on our black clothes. He couldn't figure out why, and then one day I watched him dump in the powder after the washing machine was filled with water. Novice error.

He didn't close the door even in the middle of the summer if he was coming "right back in."

The problem is that "right back in" is very loosely defined in the world of a man. Husband would go out with the intention of grabbing something from the van and coming "right back in," and then he would get distracted by something a neighbor was doing—because he's a good guy who likes to help—and that door would stay open for ten minutes or more. Our air conditioner would try to cool the entire world, but we live in Texas, and it's nearly impossible to cool just the house in the middle of summer.

"I'll do it later" didn't necessarily mean tonight.

"I'll do it later" meant a variety of things. It could be later tonight, it could be in a week, it could be next year. Later is on a sliding scale of priority—not defined by me, but defined by Husband.

Tidying up meant stacking things into piles.

Don't worry about putting it away, just simply stack it. Save yourself a little time and effort. It's taken him a while to break this habit, but I did a pretty fine job helping him break it when I fell down our stairs carrying laundry while trying to dodge a pile he'd left on the third step from the bottom. I broke my foot in that fall, and he paid the price. We had six kids, and I could no longer run after them. One man down in a house of six boys is like a suicide mission.

No more piles.

Husband's habits changed, for the most part, when we had children—and not because he finally got tired of my nagging. I finally shut up. And he realized this house would be a sinking ship without his contribution.

So thanks, babe, for stepping up your game.

How to Clean Like a Man

I'm going to tell you something that doesn't exactly make me a superwoman. But I don't care. The only thing I'll do if you put me on a pedestal is fall off. And probably break my foot while I'm at it.

Most days, once my kids are in bed and I have a little breathing room, I don't really feel like tidying up everything my kids have destroyed in the course of a day. So I don't.

But every now and then, Husband gets this irrepressible urge to clean, and, poor thing, usually acts on it while I'm stretched out in bed reading, because I'm already done for the day. His definition of cleaning, however, is not exactly my definition.

I'm not complaining here, of course. At least *somebody* is cleaning. I appreciate any and all efforts on his part, even though I would do it differently if I had the energy to pull myself out of bed.

Here's how to clean like a man.

Tidying the downstairs living areas:

Step 1: Gather everything that belongs downstairs and put it in a pile.

Step 2: Put each item in the pile in its proper place, if its proper place is downstairs.

Step 3: Gather everything that belongs upstairs.

Step 4: Pile it on the stairs.

Step 5: Leave it there. For several days. Possibly even weeks, especially if the pile includes a huge Amazon box.

Step 6: Slowly watch the pile disintegrate as your kids drag everything back into the living areas, preferably onto the floor.

Step 7: Repeat indefinitely.

Tidying the kids' playroom:

Step 1: Pile everything in the middle of the room. This makes sorting easier.

Step 2: Sort the things that are important—like guitar strings and picks and the pedal that's been missing from the keyboard piano because the toys have been holding it ransom.

Step 3: Toss everything that's not so important—like the kids' LEGO pieces or Hot Wheels cars or random pieces from a puzzle (I'm sure you'll find all the pieces eventually)—into a basket that was originally assigned to hold all the extra books.

Step 4: Put this basket somewhere kids will not be able to reach.

Step 5: Forget about it. Listen to the kids cry about how they lost their favorite car or they can't build their LEGO Starship because they can't find the steering wheel, and forget that you actually know where all of it is.

Cleaning a bathroom:

You can't even.

Sorting papers:

Step 1: Keep everything that looks important in one big pile in the corner of your room.

Step 2: Throw everything else away, even if it's an amazing artwork piece by the 4-year-old.

Tidying a master bedroom:

Step 1: Collect all the dirty dishes—from your late-night dates and restaurant order-ins that you can only manage when the kids are in bed—and put them into a box.

Step 2: Collect all the recycling in the room. Put this into a box as well.

Step 3: Collect all the trash. Put it in, you guessed it, a box.

Step 4: Don't ever move any of it. You'll take care of it tomorrow, is what you always say. And tomorrow is a slippery term.

Tidying a home library:

Step 1: Collect all the books that are not where they should be (hint: On the shelf) and stack them in a pile.

Step 2: Make sure the pile forms a tower right beside the bookshelves, where they might be shelved, eventually, but will most likely instead be spread all over the floor again by children who love to read.

Cleaning out school folders:

Step 1: Empty them.

Step 2: Put all the papers in the paper basket.

Step 3: Forget to tell your wife when there are important papers to sign.

Step 4: Let her find them a week later when one of your sons' teachers calls you to personally ask if you give permission for your son to go on a field trip.

Husband and I have been married for more than a decade. We are still learning the scientific method of tidying. But mostly we are learning the impressive difference between males and females and their definitions of tidy. He is still learning that piles don't stay piles when kids are around. I'm still learning to be grateful for living in a house with seven males.

Maybe we just need a few more years. I'm sure we can get this down soon.

Now, excuse me while I go tackle one of the piles Husband left in the living room before it becomes an explosion of papers again.

What Conversations Look Like When You're Married With Children

If you want a lesson in focus, try having a conversation with your partner while your kids are home.

At the end of every day, when Husband and I have put away our work for the evening, we try to have a quick run-down of what happened—highs and lows that we'll share, somewhat, at the dinner table but in a kid-friendly way. Husband is usually finishing up dinner and I'm usually hovering and stealing pieces of the turkey burgers he's making, while he tells me about all the contacts he made today and I tell him about all the words I wrote (one of these is clearly more interesting than the other). We're interrupted an average of forty-five times in a five-minute conversation. And when we turn our attention to the kids, usually they forget what they were going to say in the first place.

The other time that we can nearly always count on (halting) conversation is when all the kids are strapped in the car and we've turned up the radio, full blast, so we don't have to hear boys tattle. That doesn't work, of course, and oftentimes, Husband and I will wish for a police car glass separating the front seat from the back. Why aren't there cars like this made for parents yet?

In any of the instances when we think it would be a perfect time to approach a conversation, we are invariably and constantly unsuccessful.

Conversations when you're a parent really have one defining quality about them: constant interruption.

It doesn't matter at what point in the conversation you are. You could be almost all the way done with what you need to say, and miracle of all miracles no one has needed you for the last fifteen minutes—but now you've gotten to the most important part. And, of course, one of your kids will need you as soon as you start in on the finale. They will need you for the silliest of things—one will wonder how many galaxies are in the solar system, and you won't have the slightest clue. Another will need you to ask what 4,567 multiplied by 9,327 is, as if you're some kind of math whiz and didn't forget how to even add numbers after you finished your required college algebra class.

Sometimes you're interrupted because they happen to hear their name, even if they're in the middle of singing their favorite song at the top of their lungs. They will hear their name and perk up and then proceed with an interruption to ask what you're talking about. I remember my mother calling me Rabbit Ears, because I could always hear my name even when she was saying it a couple of rooms removed from mine, to someone other than me. Well, now I understand this phenomenon. I have been blessed with six rabbits, and one who will, without fail, interject into the conversation the question, "Are you talking about me?" The others, at least, will close their mouths and quietly listen.

Even if we whisper their names, they will hear it. We've done it just to test this theory. It's quite astounding, because they can't seem to hear their names when we're actually talking to them. Weird.

We've tried to teach our boys to say "Excuse me" or "Pardon me" or to wait until a break happens in the conversation to tell us what they have to say, unless, of course, it's an emergency. (The emergency definition gets a little lost in translation, too, but that's a topic for another day.) On the good days, a boy will place his hand on one of our arms and wait patiently for the talker to finish—but it is extremely hard to finish a point when you have large brown eyes staring at you like they're wondering if you're ever going to be done talking. If that doesn't steal your thought from the track down which it barreled, then you are more skilled at conversation than I am.

When you're a parent, conversations with your partner will sometimes last for days—and if you're really, really good, weeks. Sometimes you'll even think you had the conversation and you didn't at all. It was only wishful thinking. You will have mapped out the entire conversation in your head, and then on the day of your doctor's appointment, your partner will say, "I didn't know you had a doctor's appointment," and you will get mad at him, because he never listens to anything you have to say, when the real explanation is that the conversation never happened at all, except in your head. You were communicating with a figment of your own imagination.

Other times, you'll forget that you already told your partner something, and you'll delightedly repeat the same story twice, to a bored and disappointing reception.

There are so many times that I am right in the middle of saying something and one of my boys will start crying because a brother kicked his lip and made it bleed, or maybe someone just needs us to know that his poop was green today, and I can't for the life of me remember what I was saying. Have you heard the old saying "If you forget what you were trying to say, it must not have been all that important?" It turns out that if you forget what you're saying in the middle of saying it because your kids interrupted you, there is no guarantee that it is not important. I know, because none of my boys had signed permission slips for their field trips this year, because I forgot to tell their daddy they were due.

Husband and I have had the longest conversations with the fewest words while living with six boys. Here's an example of one of those conversations:

Me: Hey, I wanted to talk about the supplies that we'll need for this weekend's birthday party.

Husband: Let's make a list.

Kid 1 interruption: Mama, my brother took the ball from me.

Me: [mediating a fight over a superhero ball that is completely flat. Someone wants to play soccer with it, even though it's a flattened ball. Someone else wants to wear it as a hat. Everyone had it first.]

Fast forward half an hour.

Husband: Now what was that again?

Me: I forgot what we were talking about.

Husband: Me too.

[Collective laughter.]

Me: Oh, yeah, the birthday party.

Kid 2 interruption: Mama?

Me: I'm talking to Daddy. Just wait a minute. Don't be rude. Remember what we taught you about interrupting?

[Kid 2 places a hand on my arm and watches me intently.]

Me: I can't think. Let me just see what he wants.

[Engaged with a kid who wants to know if he can start a

business selling art. Today. Right this minute.]
    Fast forward another half hour.
    Husband: [with a good amount of sarcasm.] Back so soon?
    Me: Where were we?
    Husband: I don't think we'd even gotten started.
    Me: The birthday party. You said something about ca—
    Kid 3 interruption: Excuse me, Daddy?
    Husband: Mama and Daddy are talking. Please don't interrupt.
    [Kid 3 places a hand on Daddy's arm and watches intently for a break in the conversation.]
    Me: So cake and plates and cups.
    Husband: I'll make a list and pick some up at the store.
    Me: That would be good.
    Husband: Chocolate?
    Me: Yes. And green.
    Husband: Snacks?
    Me: Yes. And make sure the cups are recyclable.
    Husband: Got it.
    Me: One more thing—
    Kid 1 interruption: [crying] Mama, Daddy?
    Husband: Maybe we should talk later.
    Kid 1: My brother hit me.
    Husband: [turning to Kid 2] What did you want?
    Kid 2: I forgot. You were talking so long.
    Kid 1: Can we watch a movie?
    Kid 3: Did you know that a shark can smell blood from 40,000 miles away?
    When Husband and I "finish" a conversation, it's usually a day

after we actually start it, when kids are entertained out on the trampoline until someone takes a leap into someone else's knee and comes in limping to tell us all about it—with a little exaggeration thrown in for good measure.

All I know is that my focus is much more efficient now. I can keep a running commentary going in my head all day. The real challenge is remembering what I've actually said to Husband and what I've only said in my imagination.

Ah, well. Husband and I won't even finish the argument we'll have before a kid will interrupt us with a stink bomb and a proud declaration that they win the Rotten Smell Tournament.

As if one ever existed.

What Marriage Looks Like With Children

Valentine's Day for a married couple with young kids is just like any old ordinary day.

Maybe you don't think Valentine's Day is that important anyway, so this doesn't really bother you all that much. But me, well, I'll take any holiday I get to call a sitter and spend a night out with Husband so I don't have to help wrestle kids to bed. And, also, so we can enjoy a nice conversation without being interrupted every other second. But mostly so I don't have to wrestle kids to bed.

But it seems like every Valentine's Day we have a hard time trying to find a sitter. I know it's not because we have six kids and it's definitely not because we wait until Feb. 14 at 3 p.m. to make the call because I never know what day it is (Hey. A mom of young boys can hardly keep track of her kids, let alone the date.).

Plus, by the time you pay a sitter for watching your kids, there's no money left, so you'll just be walking around the neighborhood or playing a game of tennis or reclining the van seats and taking a night nap.

On second thought, that doesn't sound all that bad.

What marriage looks like with children is not anything like what I expected it would look like. I don't really know what I expected, exactly. But it wasn't this Punk'd version of life we find ourselves in today.

Husband and I are very happily married, at least most of the time—because happy is a transient state. We always work hard on our marriage, and that's really what counts.

Problem is, our kids always work hard on our marriage, too.

In case you don't know (or maybe you're wondering if you're the only one), here's what marriage looks like with children.

Date nights in bed.

Everyone's too exhausted to go anywhere anymore, so you order in, turn on Netflix's "The Newsroom," and watch while you eat. It's like a theater that serves restaurant food, except you can lie down if you want and, also, kids will burst into your room wondering what you're watching and asking if they can have a fry and why do you get to eat that food when all they had was a sandwich and raw carrots for dinner. Sometimes they'll ask you to please turn it down because it's too loud (what are they, the parents of teenagers?).

Or sometimes, instead of watching something, you read together, because it's enough being in the same room, without saying a single word, enjoying the absolute quiet that comes in the last ten minutes before you fall asleep. Sometimes you just sleep, because when all the kids are finally, finally, finally asleep, who wants to stay up till midnight knowing they'll be up at the butt crack of dawn to tell you they're starving and they're going to die if they don't have anything to eat in the next split second.

In all honesty, I enjoy the date nights in our room. I'm pretty much the biggest homebody you could ever know (biggest, as in I'd stay home for years at a time if Husband didn't drag me out, not biggest as in large. Although my kids might disagree.). Husband would go out every night of the week if he could take me with him, but I'm just not that much of a see-the-town kind of girl, after I've seen it once. He knew what he was getting into the night he proposed and I refused to go onstage at our local theatre after a beautiful production of *The Nutcracker* ballet and he had to drag me, seething, up the stairs just so he could get down on one knee. Didn't back out then. Can't back out now.

Conversation in spurts.

It's very rare that when Husband and I sit down to have a conversation we actually get to finish it. Even if the kids are all locked outside, someone will come pounding on the door to say that they need to poop or they need us to kiss a bleeding scratch or you should have heard that fart—it vibrated the whole trampoline! So, when you're married with children, you get really, really good at picking up conversations where they left off. When you're a parent, one conversation with your spouse can last whole weeks, because sometimes you forget completely what you're saying when one of the kids knocks your knees out from under you with a "What does it mean to sleep together?"

This is where date nights at home come in handy. When kids are tucked away in bed and dreaming their kid dreams, it's the perfect time to talk to each other, because no one will come knock on your door. Problem is, you have to stay awake until all the kids are asleep, and that rarely happens for us.

A fight could last forever.

Remember what I said about those conversations? Yeah, that makes fighting difficult, to say the least. We don't have any concerns about disagreeing in front of our kids, because we think it's good for them to have a healthy relationship with conflict (depending on the conflict, of course), and it's beneficial for them to witness a healthy model of conflict resolution. We have rules about arguing (no name calling, no walking away, no swearing, if we can manage. Sometimes we can't.). But if kids aren't paying the least bit of attention and they walk smack dab into the middle of a fight, asking for some milk because they're "so thirsty their mouth is dying," you'll lose your train of thought before you can even tell them they're interrupting something important. Which, in some cases, is a good thing, because most of the things we fight about are stupid anyway. Whose responsibility was it to turn on the dish washer? The kids were tardy again today because we slept an extra five minutes? Yes I did tell you this yesterday? Stupid.

Thanks, kids, for interrupting and jolting me back to reality.

Sex is…well.

Maybe you're uncomfortable with the S word. So let's just change it, for propriety's sake. Let's call it Playing Chess.

You have to know what kids will do to a chess game. It's pretty much what they do to everything they can get their hands on: deconstruct it, little by little. Right in the middle of an epic chess game, they will knock on the door to ask what day tomorrow is because they need to know if it's library day or not because that changes everything for them tonight. Sometimes you'll forget to lock the bedroom door, which is usually where you play chess, because everyone's asleep anyway, and they'll come bursting in, and you better hope you have some covers to throw over that chess game, because they're going to see something they shouldn't.ever.see.

Good luck trying to figure out what kind of move you were going to make to achieve checkmate when they've finally gone back to bed.

So, yeah, kids change a lot of things. But you know what they also do? They introduce us to a depth of love and selflessness we may never have known otherwise. Husband and I have grown to love each other more truly and deeply in these years we've been sharing the raising of our children. I understand him differently today than I understood him before kids. He understands me differently than he did before kids.

And if all this weirdness is the price we have to pay for a more passionate love all these years later, we'll surely take it.

Just remember to lock the door before you get the chess board out, m'kay?

What It's Like to Work From Home With Children

Husband and I both work from home. This is a choice we made years ago, when we found out we were expecting a child. I knew early on that I would want to work at least part of the time from home so that I could still have all the benefits of being a mother and a business woman. I love to work. I get to write a handful of essays and fiction stories that will maybe change a little piece of the world or maybe just entertain some kids for a little bit of time, and it all makes me a better mother.

When I was working for someone else, it was a bit of a stretch to convince them to let me work from home. Husband and I have always opted not to place our children in childcare, except for a brief stint with the oldest, when we thought it would be good for him to be enrolled in a preschool program. Then I decided I just wanted to teach him myself, because I thought I was qualified to teach a headstrong 4-year-old how to read and write—I was his mother, after all. I did it, too, but not without some battle scars and a threat to call the police on the kid who wouldn't sit down and copy his writing passage. That's when I knew I wasn't cut out for something like homeschool.

It was easy enough to work from home when we had one kid. It was even relatively easy with two of them. Three stretched us a little, but it wasn't *impossible*.

And then came twins.

One on five is much different than one on three. Husband and I suddenly became very inept at being the parent in charge. Fortunately, half our children are in school. But there are still twins. And twins are equivalent to having fifteen children at home.

There are so many distractions working from home.

I'm an author, which means that I require relatively calm silence. I typically wear headphones so I can't hear the circus happening downstairs while Husband is watching the kids, but there are a million ways that kids can interrupt a parent working from home.

Here are few of them:

The slam of the front and back door.

It's jarring. Husband wrote the words "Close me gently" on some masking tape and attached the same message to every surface of every door in our house—inside and outside. The boys still slam the doors. And it's not just slamming, it's SLAMMING, in a way that makes the entire house shake on its foundation. No matter how loudly I have my music turned up in my headphones, this noise shakes me out of my concentration—because the floor is moving. Is it an earthquake? Are we being bombed? Are we in the direct path of a massive tornado?

These are just a few of my thoughts when I've been jolted out of my concentration.

Maybe you should get a sturdier house, you might be thinking. Well, let me tell you. There is no house sturdy enough to withstand a boy slamming a door. Also, authors don't make a whole lot of money.

The bursting open of my bedroom door.

I work in my bedroom. I have a makeshift standing desk that is really just a dresser with a few books stacked on top of it and a laptop where I type. Yes, sometimes I freak myself out in the mirror when I accidentally catch my own eye, but that's neither here nor there. What's more freaky is when I'm fully engrossed in telling a story and the bedroom door opens and I see out of the corner of my eye, thanks to the mirror that faces the door, a form moving toward me. I go into full panic mode until I realize it's not one of my dark characters, it's one of my sons. He came to tell me that it's really hot outside. We live in Texas. It's always hot outside.

The other day my 7-year-old burst into the room—and when I say burst, you have to fully appreciate this kind of burst. It's not just an opening of the bedroom door. It's a full leaning against the door so that it crashes open. My 7-year-old happily skipped over to my side, even though I was wearing my headphones, which usually signals to any intruders that I am working and should not be disturbed. He hovered at my elbow for a few minutes, until I finally stripped the headphones off and said, "Did you need something, baby?" much more kindly than I felt.

He threw something on the dresser.

"Oh my gosh, there's a spider on your dresser," he said, with a goofy smile plastered on his face.

My heart stopped, until I saw that it was a black plastic spider and he was playing a joke on me. I shook my head, he laughed, and then he skipped out, and I had to figure out how to find my concentration again.

They will interrupt me to tell me they got to choose some random toy from their teacher's treasure box because they were really well behaved today. They'll interrupt me to tell me all about the world they built in Minecraft during their technology time today. They'll interrupt me to say they want to buy all the Pokémon cards in the world with their birthday money. Their birthday is three months away.

The cacophony of noise downstairs.

As I've already established, I work upstairs, in my bedroom. When Husband is on duty, the kids mostly keep to downstairs and the backyard. But even when they're downstairs or outside and I'm huddled away in my room, they make enough noise to still be distracting. They can do nothing without a sixophony of noise (that's a word I made up. It means the cacophony that six children can make by virtue of being in the same general location). If they're drawing, they're likely singing. If they're reading, they're likely exclaiming over something really cool. If they're having tech time, they're likely hysterically crying because they can't get Super Mario jump the way they want him to.

They're loud enough in nearly every moment to break into my consciousness. But as long as I'm not the one responsible for that noise, I can create just fine. Good thing.

Husband has suggested that maybe I should go write at a library or a coffee shop or something. But since that would require I actually get dressed, I always smile at him sweetly and say, "Thanks for the concern, babe."

One of these days I'll be a master at ignoring my distractions. Not today, but someday.

This is all practice for someday.

The Romance Equation: Keeping it Alive After Children

Before Husband and I were married, he used to do all sorts of things to romance me. He would bring me flowers and put them in beautiful vases all over my apartment so I'd remember, when I looked at them, that I was beautiful. He once gave me eleven roses instead of the full dozen and wrote me a note that said, "If you're wondering where the other rose is, just look in the mirror." I know. I'm a lucky woman.

For our first date, he showed up at my door with a handful of wildflowers, and we spent the morning at this epic mountain in Wimberley, Texas. You had to climb up five hundred sixty-three precariously wooden stairs to get all the way to the top. It was wonderful once we made it, as long as we didn't look over the side, which would make me dizzy and, because I'm one of the most graceful people on the planet, likely plummet to my death. That day he brought his guitar and we sang together, and then we kissed and then we pretended we watched the sun rise, even though the sky was covered in a cloudy haze that did not allow any sort of beauty through. The only reason we knew the sun had risen at all was that a small yellow eye hung in the clouds, and we assumed it was the muted sun.

The night he proposed to me, he went to great lengths to arrange a production with a ballet theatre that had come to town. He wanted to take me backstage and stand there, drop to one knee, and pop the question. He got all dressed up in a tux, and I wore a long and strapless red dress, and, after fighting a bit about my not wanting to go backstage because I was so incredibly hungry, he won and pulled me up on stage in front of five hundred people, dropped to a knee and, indeed, popped the question.

His romance has always been a disaster waiting to happen, but it's sweet and wonderful and so very missed.

It's a running joke in the contemporary world that once you get married—once the guy gets the girl—he stops romancing. It's not true in my case. Husband kept up his romancing for years—he crafted a life-sized card for our first anniversary, wrote a song for me on our second anniversary, and left me alone for our third anniversary.

That was the anniversary when I was eight months pregnant with our first son.

When we had children, all romancing screeched to a halt—not because he didn't want to romance me but because kids make it practically impossible to do anything special for one another.

There was the year when he tried to make me a video with the kids telling me what a great mother I was, and they just kept staring at the video camera and laughing, because they didn't know what to say and they were more interested in goofing around. There was the time when he arranged a little art project wherein they drew pictures and colored in letters and he put it all in a frame that was broken two months later by the same kids who had colored it. There was the time he tried to write me a song and then record it, and you could hear kids calling his name in the background.

No more sweet and thoughtful gifts, when you have obstacles at every turn.

He used to whisper sweet things in my ear, but it's hard to whisper anything sweet when there's a kid pulling on your arm, trying to demand your attention. Most days, our sweet whisperings sound like any of these phrases:

"Hey, do you want me to wash the dishes tonight? I know you have book club."

"I made the bed today, and I put a load of laundry in the wash. Just thought you should know."

"How about I take the kids to the pool for the evening and you stay here and…clean up?"

Once, on a Mother's Day after I'd just had twins, Husband left me a note and said, "I thought you might enjoy a day off from church." He'd left all the kids home with me, because he also thought I'd like to spend Mother's Day with them.

Well, he had good intentions, at least.

"Why don't you go to the grocery store by yourself, honey?" is also a frequent romancing technique, even though going to the grocery store is probably the last thing I'd like to do, because it requires too much thinking, since I nearly always leave my list at home. I usually take him up on it, though, because at least I'm getting out of the house. Sometimes I'm so tired I can hardly move, and a vegetative state without kids jumping on me every five minutes is preferable to going out to the grocery store, but I'll still do it, because "a vegetative state without kids jumping on me every five minutes" is not an actual possibility in our house.

As you can imagine, Husband and I also don't get very many

date nights out. It's not easy to find a sitter for six kids, especially when you're calling at the last minute. So our romancing looks like sharing a bowl of popcorn in our bed while we catch up on Netflix shows.

Romancing looks a lot different now that we have kids. It looks more like completely tidying the house before I come down from a long day at work. It looks like playing a game of trampoline dodgeball with the boys out back so I can have a few minutes to myself while I wash the dishes. It looks like distracting kids with a story while I squeeze in a five-minute shower.

But you know what? All of that is romantic, too, because these are acts of sacrifice. Maybe there isn't a whole lot I can show for it—there's not a love song I can sing in the shower or a video I can share with all my family or a card that I can keep in my dresser forever. But that does not diminish the romance of these small and thoughtful acts.

Romance is all how you look at it.

And, if I'm being honest, the small and thoughtful acts mean more to me. Sure, it was fun to get all dolled up so I could stand on a theatre stage and cry my yes to his question. Sure, it was exciting to see him show up at my door with a bouquet of random flowers hiding his face and then follow him out to watch the sunrise. Sure, it was wonderful to be called a beautiful rose.

But we get to do interesting things now, too. We get to curl up in a blanket on a winter morning and watch the sunrise from the back porch while the kids are still (hopefully) sleeping. We get to drink hot chocolate in the late hours of the night and eat popcorn and watch old episodes of "How I Met Your Mother." We get to share our lives with children and watch them enrich it with beauty and meaning.

The other day Husband brought me flowers for the first time in years. He put them on a table and all the boys exclaimed over them, pointing out their colors and their shapes and the water that would keep them alive, at least for a few days. The whole kitchen seemed brighter, and I smiled.

It's still possible to romance after children. You just have to know what you're looking for.

The Truth About Missing the Before-Children Days

Every now and then, Husband and I get a glorious weekend to ourselves. We will split up the boys (because neither of our parents can handle six at a time. Don't know why.) and send them away with the grandparents.

It's glorious, because we get to remember what it's like to finish an entire sentence without being interrupted by a kid who wants to tell me about all his Minecraft plans for the next three years. We get to enjoy what it's like to wrap our arms around each other without a cute little toddler begging to join in the fold because he just tried to walk down the last stair like a big person, and he landed on his head. We can eat the bad-for-us food right out in the open instead of hidden behind the locked door of our bedroom, with all the wild animals sniffing around outside in the hall, begging for "just one little taste."

We live for these weekends.

As you might have guessed, they don't come as often as we would like. This is mostly because there are six kids and they're all young and they have lots of energy and grandparents are old (sorry, Mom). And I'll go ahead and say it: boys are really tough. At the end of most days I feel like I've been run over by a UPS truck on its way to deliver someone else's chocolate, and those are the *good* days. The bad days? I'd liken myself to the Wicked Witch flattened beneath a house, about to get her shoes stolen.

These are compelling reasons why, every now and then, I need a break.

Sometimes, though, schedules don't work out or people are busy, and Husband and I can go long, long stretches of time without any sort of relief. No date nights, no lone grocery trip out, no magical kid-less weekends. And sometimes, when those stretches come and it feels like I have to scrape myself out of bed with a spatula called Exhaustion, I'll find myself in this dark and dreary place where I start missing what it was like to be a married couple without children.

No one really talks about this dark and dreary place. It's far too taboo in our society—not because it doesn't happen for nearly everyone (Perfect Parents are excluded from these I Miss the Before-Children Days, because we know they are perfect and they never ever think about what life was like before a 4-year-old figured out how to rip a parent's arm out of socket by executing a perfect twist-flip when the parent carried him kicking and screaming from the park). No one really talks about this dark and dreary place because no one likes to admit that it exists.

Well, it does.

And here's the thing: Admitting that you miss the Before-Children Days doesn't make you an ungrateful parent. It makes you human. We're inclined to prefer what's easiest, and even if we didn't recognize it before we had children, the Before-Children Days were pretty easy compared to these days, when we're up all night feeding a baby who refuses to sleep and then we're arguing every other minute with a strong-willed toddler and then we're trying to convince a headstrong preteen that he does need a bath, we can smell him from a football field away—what's he wearing, Sweaty Dog with a side of Sour Armpit?—and then we're working to keep our heart steady during the raising of a teenager with a driver's license and then we're trying to let them go off on their own as a young adult, hoping, hoping, hoping we did our job.

None of it is easy. Some of it will make us say, *What have we done?*

I hardly remember the Before-Children Days. They seem so long ago. Children change a life in such a drastic way that you don't really remember what came before them. They steal the show. The only thing I know for sure is that Husband and I didn't enjoy the alone time we had together as much as we should have—as much as we might have had we known what the future would look like.

Here are the things I miss most:

1. Eating a whole meal without having to get up. Or share.

When the time comes to sit down and have dinner as a family, I can guarantee that I will forget to bring something to the table. One of my boys will remind me I forgot it as soon as I take my first bite of food. It's so predictable. Sometimes I delay that first bite, until I'm sure no one is missing anything, and then, as soon as that roasted chicken hits my tongue, one of the 4-year-olds will say, "You forgot to get me some milk." Get it yourself, I'd like to say, except my twins are like wrecking balls, ready and willing to do everything themselves but not quite good at it yet. I know that if I invite them to get their own milk, they'll gladly do it, but I will not gladly accept the consequences of this allowance.

As soon as I give them their glasses of milk, I'll sit down and put bite number 2 in my mouth, and this one no sooner passes my lips when someone else will remind me that we don't have any napkins, and since no one cares as much as I do about wiping hands on shirts, I'm usually the one who has to get up and locate where Husband put all the cloth napkins this time—because the storage place is different every week. Not intentionally. He's scatter-brained and forgets that they actually have a designated place. That's okay. I'll spend the next five minutes on a treasure hunt, trying to unlock the workings of Husband's mind while my food grows colder and colder.

I'll sit back down, and someone will mention that we don't have the salt and the chicken is tasteless (thanks, kid), and since the salt was moved to a cabinet where no child could reach it after I discovered the 4-year-olds emptying the grains into their mouth, I have to get it. Then someone will need more green beans because he's already finished with his first round and someone else will need more chicken and someone else will need a fork, because whoever set the table miscounted, and, you know, I'm already up.

I also miss being able to eat my restaurant leftovers without having kids gather around asking for bites and sticking their fingers in my jalapeño ranch dip for a little taste. Get thee gone, carrion.

Other things that would be nice to add to the Perfect Mealtime list: Getting through an entire meal without someone complaining about what's for dinner, surviving broccoli cheese soup night without a vomit joke, and finishing any dinner where boys don't move from their places a billion times.

2. Getting into the car effortlessly.

Right now getting into the car requires endless effort. I miss the days when all Husband and I had to do was decide to go somewhere, and we got in the car and left. It takes us an average of half an hour to leave our house with all these boys in tow, even if we're only visiting the Target that's 2.5 miles away. Inevitably, someone will forget their shoes or someone else will decide he needs to go potty (usually number two), and someone else will, at the last minute, decide that he needs a thousand books to take with him to the park.

We've never gotten farther than our neighborhood entrance before someone shouts out, "I forgot (fill in the blank)." Shoes. Pants. Or, God forbid, underwear.

3. Going any place we want.

Kids are quite picky about where they want to spend their days. I haven't been to an art museum in years—although, I have to admit, that's not so much because the kids haven't asked but because every time I think about being in an art museum with all those ancient masterpieces and two 4-year-old twins who are masters at escaping, doing their own thing, and, mostly, destruction, I shiver a little. So we stick to the safer destinations, like the zoo, where they could crawl into a crocodile exhibit without my noticing, or the children's museum, where they can climb to the top of a tower and call it exploring. This, of course, limits our fun day possibilities, but at least I don't have to watch a classic Monet get knocked and dragged around and attempt to pretend that's not my kid destroying it.

Every now and then, though, I wish I could go, just once, wherever it is I want to go, without worrying that someone will be bored out of his mind or someone will surely destroy the place or someone will probably complain about being there the entire time.

4. Staying up as late as we want.

On the rare occasion that Husband and I get a date night, we rarely stay out past ten. This is mostly because our bedtime is about

9 o'clock sharp. Anytime after that, our mental and physical capabilities start to shut down. But I've noticed that on the weekends we spend sans kids, we might stay up until 2 in the morning, no problem, and we'll feel it the next day, but *we can still do it*. So we're not entirely old. We're just parents. Parents whose kids come knocking on the door at 5 a.m. to tell us we have to get up. On weekends without kids, we don't ever go to bed before midnight. We stay up doing things like organizing our bedroom and cleaning out our garage, because we're super interesting people like that.

5. Going anywhere without thinking of the kids.

For our tenth anniversary, Husband and I revisited the place where we honeymooned—the magical Disney World. We had a grand time when we were 21 and 22, and we thought we'd have just as grand a time for our tenth anniversary. The problem was that everything we saw would make us think of the kids. We kept thinking about how the oldest one would really like that treehouse and the second-in-line would really like that teacup ride, and the third son would have loved the pirate boat. We wished we could show them this and that. We wished they were with us so we could experience it all over again through their eyes.

I know that if we'd had them there with us, we probably would have been wishing we'd been able to come alone, because such is life.

Whenever Husband and I start missing the good old days, something will inevitably catch our eyes, and we'll think of our children. "He would like that," we'll say, and then we'll look at each other and laugh a little.

Those Before-Children days often look attractive and glamorous. But not every day. And the days when they don't, they only look lonely. Our boys have grown into a large and luminous space in our lives, and we'll never be the same.

As it should be.

How Children Change a Life Dream

Before we became parents, Husband and I were in a band. We're still in a band—it's just that we never really seem to scrape up enough energy to get out and play.

Back then, though, we wanted to be rockstars. We wanted to play in packed theaters for sold-out crowds that knew all our songs by heart. We dreamed of touring and writing songs every day and recording them all in the studio every year and then listening to their genius on the radio.

Then came kids.

We got three albums under our belt before six kids came along. We've been working on a fourth album for six years now.

It's not easy to pursue a dream when you have kids. Before kids, it wasn't ever a problem to take a week off work, pack up for a midwestern tour and pull all-nighters in a Honda Odyssey on the way to the next show in another state. We could easily spend a week laying down tracks and belting lyrics into a microphone (liquored up, if you're me—that recording is FOREVER, and that's a lot of pressure for a perfectionist).

Now it's much more complicated. We either have to find someone to take care of the kids for that whole entire week (which isn't easy, trust me), or we just take them with us, which sounds like a living nightmare to me. Our last recording trip happened six years ago, two weeks after our third son was born. I had three boys 3 years old and younger. It might not have been real fun, but it was definitely real. Constant diaper changes, 3 a.m. feedings, a billion battles over cleanup, and then Husband would come home and say, "Okay, it's your turn to lay down the bass and vocals." I couldn't even remember what my name was, let alone how to play a B flat on the bass guitar.

Husband and I used to be able to play in restaurants and bars and coffeeshops around town without worrying about that thing called Logistics, but now it's like planning for a high-security prison break just to get out the door. We used to be able to set up and sing without a whole bunch of extra hands trying to "help" and really just tangling cords. We used to be able to play a two-hour set without worrying who had which kid and where the youngest went when the babysitter wasn't watching.

We tried to keep at it for a while. And then we got a little burned out, because the universe (and by universe, I mean kids) seemed to be working wholeheartedly against us.

And you know what? That's okay. Because the thing about kids and circumstances and all these challenges that make chasing a dream seem completely and ridiculously impossible is that they show us *how much we really want it.*

So maybe we can't play live gigs anymore, at least for a while. That doesn't mean we have to pack up our instruments and call it a day for the rest of our lives. So maybe we can't seem to get an entire album recorded in the course of a year. Well, the marketplace has changed, which means we can get a single finished and still share it with the world. So maybe we don't get to do this as often as we'd like. **We still get to do it.** And sometimes our kids even get to see us do it.

Every now and then I find myself wondering if maybe it's selfish to consider chasing my dream—writing essays and stories and songs and sharing them all with the world. I'm a parent, after all. Shouldn't I just be content with parenting while my kids are young? They won't always be young.

It's a complicated thing, but the truth is that chasing my dreams makes me a better person. It shows me who I can be. It nurtures my heart and my mind, both of which need to be healthy in order to be a good parent.

And that's not all. Chasing my dreams also helps me teach my kids that it's still possible to do what you've always dreamed of doing after you have a family. Life doesn't end with kids. It actually begins in a brand new, deeper way. I wouldn't trade that for the world.

Parents might have to pursue their dreams in the slim little margins of life, but it is still possible. It doesn't always look perfect. Sometimes we get frustrated about the lack of time. Sometimes we feel really burned out, because we're working so hard at everything. Sometimes we stay up way too late and get up way too early.

But it's important for Husband and me to show our boys that a family doesn't eliminate a dream—it just changes it a little. We are meant to live a life of passion and pursuit, and that's what our children learn every time they look at us and see how hard we work chasing something as seemingly reckless as recording songs or writing a book or inventing that thing we always wanted to see out in the marketplace.

What my boys are learning every time they look at their daddy and me, every time they hear us talk about the music we miss, every time we have the pleasure of getting up on a stage and playing our hearts out is that *anything is possible, if you work hard enough.* A dream doesn't just happen. You have to work relentlessly hard at it. That's a powerful lesson for them to learn.

They're talking about starting their own band now, which is the secret reason we had so many (do you know how much money boy bands make?). Most people think we had so many because we wanted a basketball team with a sub. The last time I tried to play basketball, I jammed four fingers and got a bloody nose, and I'm pretty sure that my boys got most of my athletic genes.

Music and dance lessons, here we come.

The Importance of Time Off When You're a Mother

A few years ago, when I was feeling completely exhausted from being a mother and was desperate to take a break—however short it was—from all the responsibilities, right around the time I started also feeling guilty for feeling exhausted because other mothers did it, and why couldn't I, I picked up Susan Cain's book, *Quiet: The Power of Introverts in a World That Can't Stop Talking*, and started reading.

The book was about me. This was completely surprising.

It could be because I'd spent the last several years working as a journalist—during which I had to interact with people on a regular and hourly basis—but I had no idea that I was an introvert. Cain's book showed me that I was not just an introvert, I was a introverted mother living in a house that practically shakes itself apart with constant noise and always-present people. I was an introverted mother who did not take nearly enough time to recover from such an energy-draining life.

As a mother, I often feel overcome with guilt for needing to take some time away from my children. I forget that I matter, too.

In the daily realities of life, children demand so much. They ask us to constantly be there, constantly meet their needs, constantly engage in conversation (if you have a 9-year-old Motor Mouth like I do), and sometimes just keeping up with all the ideas they have in a day makes me want to go to sleep. Come dinner time, I've lost my capacity to make any sort of decision, because my brain is so frazzled from diffusing arguments, pouring milk, wiping noses, kissing hurts, changing diapers, pretending like I'm listening to an endless Minecraft monologue and then, when all those responsibilities are put on pause for a few hours, I spend the rest of the afternoon writing my heart out on a page.

I say all the time that my work is my respite, but the truth is that work is not enough of a respite—because I'm still creating for other people, still telling my stories to bring hope and joy and knowledge and entertainment to the lives of others. Which means at the end of the day, I still need time that's just for me, time that does not have any requirements attached to it, time in which I can hear myself think and breathe.

This is not selfish. It's necessary.

If I don't take the necessary time away from responsibilities and people, I feel on edge, panicked, exhausted. You can't parent well when you feel on edge, panicked, exhausted. You can only parent defensively. Tiredly. Bitterly.

I am overstimulated on a daily basis. There are boys yelling at each other over the LEGO piece they all wanted, and above the noise, someone is asking if they can have a glass of milk early, instead of with dinner. And someone else is hollering about how their brother bounced on their head while they were all playing on the trampoline, and someone else is hanging on my arm, trying to tell me about his day at school. Someone else is talking about how his brother hit him when he wouldn't give back a Pokémon card he'd stolen.

During these times I will look around my house, my heart thundering in my chest because when six people are talking to me at the same time, it feels like danger. I can't escape, though, because not only am I in charge, but there are booby traps all over the room. I would break a leg if I tried to run from the tornadoes sucking me into their vortex.

Of course there's never a good time to hide myself away. They always come looking. And if they don't come looking, that's even worse. I'll likely unlock the bathroom door, where I've been sitting on the toilet reading a *National Geographic* article, and they will have wrapped the living room with eco-friendly paper towels and thread from the sewing machine I left out. Thanks, kids.

Husband can usually tell when I'm about to break. He's a good husband. He'll tell me, "Go sit out for five minutes," and I'll agree. I'll fully recognize that I'm not going to make it without these few minutes away, but that doesn't stop the guilt from climbing up the stairs with me and sneaking into my room before I can close the door in its face.

The problem is that we are taught to believe that good mothers don't need breaks from their children. We are taught that we can do everything. We are taught that time away is for terrible mothers.

If I don't take time away, however, my children are not getting the best version of their mother. And this, in the end, is much more important than adhering to some ridiculous societal expectation.

Not only that, but when I take time to myself, I inadvertently teach my boys that it's okay to take time to themselves and it's okay, should they choose to marry, for their partners to take time off.

What their daddy is teaching them in his daily help is that parenting is a shared experience. What I am teaching them in my time off is that everyone—including mothers—need time to themselves.

So, on that note, I think I'll go soak in a lavender bath and read a book.

How to Turn Family Dinners into Family Gag Fests

Craziness—it's what's for dinner.

I used to have these grand notions about what dinner would look like when I had a family of my own. I grew up in a home where my mother tried as hard as she could to get us all to sit down at the same time and eat. It worked until we became busy teenagers involved in anything and everything.

I knew, early on, that I wanted to demand sit-down dinners with my own children.

There is something special about a shared dinner. We get to be silly, we get to sometimes talk about something serious, we get to have meetings if so we desire (you can hear our kids complain about these long and boring meetings every Sunday evening at 6 p.m.). I love family meals.

But it must be said that I had some expectations going in that were obliterated pretty quickly. I envisioned our family, gathered around the table, sitting calmly, talking about our days and listening attentively to one another. And it's true that our dinners started out that way, when there was only one child and he couldn't yet talk, but things have become a little more, well, complicated.

What it really boils down to is this: I would like to make it through one dinner without feeling like I need to throw up.

It's not the food. Husband is a great cook. He does most of the cooking, because I'm not very good at it. I'll cook when I have to, of course, but it'll be a sparse night if they let me light the burners. Husband loves me for other reasons. We've both known this all along. The first time I baked him a birthday cake for his twenty-first birthday and it fell apart while he was cutting it gave him the necessary clues that I was no expert in the kitchen. And he still married me. You get what you get, and you don't throw a fit.

All that to say Husband mostly assumes this chef role in the kitchen, and he's impressively experimental, much to my delight and my boys' consternation. We never know what's for dinner, even after we taste it. We just know it's good, not gross.

Gross comes in the form of six little boys.

It's not that they're *trying* to be gross. It's just that, predictably I suppose, right around the time we take our first or second bite, someone will secretly let loose an SBD (Silent But Deadly, a modifier of the word "fart," for those of you who are not as familiar with this wonder of nature), and it will stink up the whole entire room so that not only are my nose hairs completely singed, but I can't taste my food, because my taste buds have shriveled up in an effort to avoid whatever it is my brain has signaled I'm about to put in my mouth— which is not the SBD, but try explaining that to your brain.

Or, if no one has an entertaining case of gas, one of the boys will talk about the bug he accidentally squished under his shoe on the playground today and will finish off this remarkably detailed story in which bug legs are splayed out on the pavement with a "Did you know that a cricket's blood is yellow? See?" He will hold up his shoe, where there's still a severed leg attached to the mush, and I will vomit a little in my mouth.

If that doesn't happen, someone else will feel so proud about the thing he did in school today, which he forgot to tell me about before he stuffed a large glob of roast in his mouth, that he will have to tell me right now. But rather than saying it, he will spray it. All over the mashed potatoes I was about to put on my plate. Stir it around, make it disappear, extra seasoning. Out of sight, out of mind.

Turns out that saying's not true in the slightest, but thanks for the false hope.

Sometimes, if I'm really fortunate, Husband gets in on the act, too. He has this thing about popping pimples, which means any time there's a new video on the Internet that shows someone popping a pimple and all the junk that oozes out, he can't NOT watch it. Which means he'll tell me all about it. Over dinner.

Romantic, I know.

We try really hard to teach our boys about proper manners and how to act when a lady is present, but try as we might, they don't see me as a lady, only Mama. This could have something to do with the fact that I hold the title for Best Burper in the House, but still. I'm a lady.

Most of their gross contributions at dinnertime are innocent. It's not like they're scheming beforehand, whispering into their boy circle, "How can we gross Mama out at dinner tonight?" It's just that the dinner table is the place where we all get to sit down and talk, and it's the only time in our schedule when any one kid will have our undivided attention, at least until their snuggle time. So the 9-year-old thinks it's important to tell me that while he was walking home with his friend today, he stepped in a massive pile of dog poop, and it was still fresh. The 7-year-old will tell me about the person who blew his nose in music class today and ended up with a handful of gooey green snot. The 6-year-old will tell me about the dead frog they found, also on the walk home from school today, and how he picked it up and threw it in a trash can—and, no, he didn't wash his hands after that.

And let's not even mention the kid who will tell me all about the spider that dropped from the ceiling onto his lap while he was doing homework IN MY CHAIR and how he decided to just let it crawl away instead of killing it.

For once, I'd like to eat my dinners without feeling the need to gag.

But I suppose that soon enough they'll be running off to have dinner with friends, or, God help us, girls, and we won't be able to sit down as often as we do now and enjoy the gross conversation around a hot, satisfying meal. So I'll just enjoy my gross dinners, with my intermittent pleas for them to remember their manners.

And maybe, if we're lucky, the gross talk will keep the girls away for a while.

How to Be a Mother of Boys

11 Mom Looks that are Familiar to Boys

There are certain instances where I have only to look at my boys for them to know, without any word spoken, that they will pay for this, that they should stop doing whatever it is they're doing, and that I am quite annoyed with their choices, among other subtle communication clues. These looks come in handy when I'm on the phone with a doctor's office trying to schedule their appointments and I don't want to cover the mouthpiece and yell at them to stop swinging on the fan. They come in handy when I'm in the middle of a conversation and I don't want to be rude, but I do want them to stop climbing over chairs like they're monkeys. They come in handy when I'm dropping my older boys off at school and a teacher stops us to ask how everyone's doing and I would like them to stop doing "the worm" on the floor of an elementary school in which thousands of kids daily wipe their snot on their hands and then touch everything.

Every time I turn a Mom Look on one of my boys, their eyes widen a little bit and they quickly shape up.

Mom looks can communicate many things.

1. I know what you're thinking, so don't even think about it.

This is the most frequent Mom Look I use when I'm having a conversation with another person. My boys believe that because I'm engaged with another person, I'm not paying any attention them. The truth is that I'm on hyper-alert when I'm on the phone, because

I know what they'll likely try, and not all of it will be as simple as stealing some forbidden cookies.

This Mom Look also comes in handy when we're in the park and I don't want to yell at my kids in front of all the people there, especially his potential friends and the woman who just came up to talk to me. So I turn this Mom Look on the kid who's about to put his brother, who can barely walk, on the monkey bars.

2. What in the world were you thinking?

I try really hard to be empathic when it comes to my boys getting hurt. But when they run inside with a whole half of their leg scraped off and they tell me that they were trying to ride two scooters down the hill like skates and they face planted halfway down, this is the Look I pull out. I know they can decode this Look, because I can see the way their face gets confused for a minute, which tells me exactly what I thought: they were, to put it simply, not thinking at all.

They also get this Look leveled at them when they come in with a flaming red mark on the side of their face and tell me they were sword fighting with shovels but they didn't quite aim right and their brother nearly took off their head.

And, again, when they confess that they just broke a light because they were trying to perfect a soccer head butt in the house.

3. You're in big trouble now, mister.

This Look comes around when the boys are out playing and they've just broken one of the neighbor's garden decorations, even though they weren't supposed to play with them in the first place. It comes around when they pick the lock on their bedroom door with the shard of a hanger they smuggled in their blanket and then waited until the opportune moment for their escape presented itself, when they thought for sure I wouldn't be standing guard (I almost always am, twins.). It comes around when they shove three pounds of grapes in their kissers and then complain of a tummy ache.

It also comes around when they take one of my writing notebooks and try to practice writing their name, even though they don't really know how to hold a pencil yet or spell their name. And, my favorite, it comes around when they wander off in the store while I'm reading labels trying to decide which peanut butter is healthier and I spend the next twenty minutes locked in a panic attack because someone surely took them, since they're super cute, if somewhat maddening.

4. I wish I didn't want to laugh right now.

I try my hardest not to laugh when my kids say or do something inappropriate. Like the other day, when my 7-year-old admitted to me that sometimes when he's trying to run, he trips over his legs. He said it deadpan-style, and I knew he was serious, because he really does have a problem sometimes when he gets going too fast. He has long, skinny legs that he hasn't quite grown into. I had to try my best not to laugh.

When the 9-year-old gets really upset at his daddy and tells him that Daddy owes him thirty dollars for being mean to him (mean, meaning, not giving him what he wants), I try not to laugh. When the 6-year-old says he had a nightmare about his twin brothers breaking into his room and stealing his LEGO mini figures, I have to try not to laugh.

The boys know they're amusing, and sometimes this can cut tension. But sometimes it just makes them madder to hear me laugh, so I have to try really, really hard. That's where the Look comes in.

5. If looks could kill you'd be buried ten feet deep.

This Look usually settles upon them when they do something they're not supposed to do—something they've likely been told several times that they're not supposed to do. Most recently this Look came to visit when the 4-year-olds played with the plunger, sloshing poop water all over the bathroom, and when I went into the bathroom, I slipped and fell into it. (My life is like a bad cartoon where I'm the person my boys are always torturing).

This Look descends upon them when Husband tells me that they've done something like peed in the brand new air conditioner unit out back, or they've left one of my writing notebooks out in the rain and I can't read the last sixty days of poems I wrote, or one is trying to smuggle a toy into bed that he'll use later to break out of his room so he can wander in the middle of the night while everyone is sleeping and guzzle another vial of essential oil.

7. Stop it. Now.

This Look is usually reserved for places like church and the playground and doctor's offices, where I can't really speak freely or loudly in the way I normally do. I just level a Look at them. Sometimes, if they're feeling really brave, they'll pretend they don't see it, and then I'll pretend, when we get home, that the sun has already set and it's time for bed. Other times it works like a charm, as in the instance when one of my 4-year-olds picked up a fallen branch at the local park and started to swing it at his twin brother's face. He dropped that branch real quick when the Look connected with his eyes.

I use this Look when my boys are getting ready to dump out a whole box of crayons, when one of them is about to color all over the drawing their older brother did, when someone's raiding the fridge even though they had a snack three minutes ago, and when they're flipping off the couch—as in, literally flipping—among many, many, many other instances.

8. When I get off this phone, you better run.

My boys are pretty big opportunists. So when I'm talking on the phone—which isn't often, by the way. I only use the phone when I absolutely need it—they use every trick in their book. One of them will steal upstairs, forgetting that this is a mobile phone and I can chase him every bit of the way. Another will try to escape out the front door, thinking I won't hear the slam of it and come barreling out myself. Another will open up the disastrous game closet that I tidied six months ago and pull out only the games with a thousand pieces, fully believing that I will not see these when he leaves them out to puncture the soft parts of my feet. Another will attempt to kick a soccer ball in the house, miss, send his shoe flying and land flat on his back with the air knocked out of him. I level this Look on him just for good measure, even though he got exactly what he deserved.

9. Get back in your room.

This Look, as you might imagine, is usually reserved for the nighttime hours in our house. They pretend that they're trying to sleep, but really they're just waiting for us to disappear into our room so they can tromp out to the bathroom and press their butt cheeks to the mirror or make art on the counter with toothpaste so they can then lick it up or simply practice perfecting their arc-stream into the toilet, which has yet to happen, by the way. Sometimes I wish I could become a hologram and send this Look beaming through the doors and hovering in the hall so they wouldn't even think about getting out of bed.

10. Too many words. System malfunction.

Every evening, right around dinner time, I have reached my full quota of words. The thing about six children is that there are so many words, all at the same time. If there's anything that makes a mother feel overwhelmed, it's six children talking to her simultaneously. I can't decode that kind of talk. So most of the time, I'll level this Look at them, which never works. Then I'll pretend I'm a robot and start repeating "System malfunction" in a monotone robot voice. In very rare cases it doesn't come to that. The 9-year-old surprised me the other day by saying, "Hey, guys, be quiet. It looks like Mama has reached her capacity."

Smart boy, that one.

And probably the most frequent Mom Look leveled on my children is this one:

11. I'm so proud to be your mama.

Their very existence stirs feelings of pride and joy. I am proud to call them my sons, I am proud to call them amazing human beings, I am proud to call them a representative of my name and that of my husband, even when they're picking their boogers and eating them.

So I plaster this Look on my face like a silly fool as often as I can so they know I love them to pieces.

8 Ridiculous Things About Which I No Longer Care

It's taken me nine years of resistance, but I have officially passed into the territory of A Parent Who Doesn't Care.

I'm mostly talking about the way I look. Tell me, please, who in the world has time to care about the way she looks when one boy is flying off the trampoline with a towel he thinks will work as a parachute and another is rummaging through his daddy's locked shed—he already picked the lock—and taking out a massive chain saw that he'll race around the yard along with an accompanying roar, which is, presumably, the sound he thinks a chainsaw would make. Another is asking for his fourteenth snack of the afternoon.

I don't have time to care. Sorry, Husband. You're lucky if I smell nice anymore.

Here are some things that have gone down the drain since becoming a parent of six boys:

My hair.

I used to have great hair. I remember a time when I would actually curl it with hot rollers. I always liked to wear my hair long for this very purpose—those beautiful auburn curls etching their natural flourishes onto my shirt. I still wear my hair long, but I never do anything with it, so it just lies sad and flat or, usually, gets tied back into ponytail. Also, my gray hairs have multiplied exponentially since becoming the mom of twins. And because I'm a tree hugger sort, I won't be dyeing it until there's an eco-friendly alternative.

My attire.

I wear what I like to affectionately call a Mama Uniform. It is, at its simplest, a pair of workout pants, a sports bra, a T-shirt, and my running shoes. I joke with the people who ever dare to say anything that I wear these clothes because my boys keep me on my feet and running in all directions. This is true—when I'm on duty, I hardly get to sit down for five minutes before someone is doing something that they didn't fully think through when the idea came crashing into their brains—like riding a bike with a blindfold. Being pre-prepared in workout clothes and running shoes means that I will be ready, at a moments' notice, to race out the doors when someone thinks it would be a good idea to drop their drawers and water the plants from the top of our van.

Sometimes I accessorize this Mama Uniform with a black sweatshirt, which takes attention off the many stains my workout shirts wear because kids like to use me as their napkin, their snot rag, their pillow and, of course, their vomit shield.

My smooth limbs.

I've grown so used to walking around my house wearing shorts even though I haven't shaved my legs that once I accidentally walked all the way to my boys' school before I realized I'd ventured outside with man calves visible to the world. Sorry you had to see that, world. And yet I'm not sorry. A woman should be able to show her hair if she wants to. Who got to decide that a beautiful woman was only the one with perfectly smooth legs? I wasn't on the council, and I'd like to revoke the decision. If I want to walk around with porcupine quills growing out of my legs, just give me a wide berth, please.

My perfectly bagless eyes.

Once upon a time, when I did not have any children, I used to take spoons out of my freezer and apply them to my eyes every morning. I'd read in a beauty magazine that this got rid of the bags under your eyes. I didn't care if it was true. I just did it.

Now, however, I don't even bother, because it's just another step to a morning routine that includes fixing breakfast, waking up boys (multiple times), reminding boys to put folders in backpacks (multiple times), pouring milk, washing out bowls, changing a baby's diaper, and shouting over the noise that it's time to leave (multiple times). If you read carefully, you'll notice a theme here.

If I were to add this step to my morning routine, it would mean emerging from my room, which has a squeaky door, at 4:15 and attempting to slip past my boys' rooms without waking them. Every parent knows that as soon as a kid smells you awake, he's awake, too. And I'd like my two hours of alone time. So I skip the frozen spoons. And you can tell. But I don't care.

My shoes.

Yes, those are holes in my shoes, thanks for noticing. I haven't bought myself new clothes or shoes in three years. That's about the time when I added my twins to the mix of little boys. They terrorize clothes just like they terrorize everything else in the world, so all our clothes budget goes to keeping our twins clothed.

One of these days, I'll buy myself something new. For the next seventeen years, I might be wearing holey shoes.

The swimsuit.

I used to be all about the bikini. Not string bikinis or anything wild, because I've always been a modest person, mostly because I've never been truly comfortable with my body.

But you would not want to see me in a bikini now. Six children do a number on the belly, and I'm not just talking about the baby weight. There are also stretch marks and the umbilical hernia I had to repair after my twins and what happens when you go through another pregnancy with a piece of mesh holding your insides together. Also, there was an emergency appendectomy in there somewhere, so let's just say that a two-piece is not in my future any longer. And I'm doing the world a favor.

The made up face.

There was a time when I would not think about going anywhere without makeup on. Now I can hardly think of going anywhere *with* makeup on. This is because makeup takes much too long to apply. In the ten minutes I apply my makeup, my boys can cover every available window space on our van with stickers, can rearrange all the books on our library shelves (and by rearrange I mean take them all off and get too tired to put them back on), and consume two pounds of apples. So no thanks.

Husband told me the other day that he wants to start doing more video marketing with one of our parenting platforms, and I groaned, because that means I'll have to actually put on makeup. He asked why that means I had to put on makeup—couldn't I just do it like I would normally look? I couldn't stop laugh-crying. Because no. No one wants to see this face on camera without makeup.

The wrinkles.

Nope. I still care about those.

(But there are a lot more now. I blame the kids. And the crying at night over my challenging life. Just kidding. I don't cry. I just complain.)

I don't really care about the way I look or the way I smell or the way I dress—whether or not I come across as one of those moms who has it all together. The truth is, at the end of the day—or the beginning of the day—I'm just too tired to care.

My kids think I'm beautiful. A little overweight, a little uncool, a little old, but mostly beautiful. Husband just thinks I'm beautiful.

And that's all that really matters.

5 Important Things I've Learned From My Boys

As parents, we sometimes think that we're supposed to know everything there is to know about life and kids and especially raising children. But in the nine years I've spent parenting, there are still some places I come up against where I feel completely out of my league.

The other day, my 8-year-old asked me how women have babies —mostly because he recently got a new baby brother, and all he remembers is Mama going to the hospital with a big belly and coming home with a new baby (and still a big belly).

I have no idea how to talk to my boys about sex and babies and things like puberty and wet dreams and all the things we don't really consider when the nurses put those precious little newborns into our arms.

But what I've learned in all these years is that, often, our children help us through these shaky places. Of course I've learned much from Husband and other parents and reading books, but these little people living in my home have taught me valuable things, too.

They have taught me:

1. There is no such thing as hurry.

Whether we are painfully late or satisfactorily early, my children move at the same exact speed. Which is maddeningly slow. No amount of "hurry up" speak will make them move any faster, either. And, as annoying as it is sometimes, I'm glad. Their inability to move at a hurried pace is refreshing, because so much of the time I am racing from one thing to another, trying to put the laundry in the wash and make sure their breakfast stays hot and turning on the light in the bathroom for my toddlers, and everything is always hurry, hurry, hurry, or we won't have time for it.

2. You can still do what you love in the margins.

When I became a mother, I stopped writing. Life was just so busy, and I worked a full-time job and I wanted to spend all my extra time with my boys. But I abandoned the pursuit of something I really loved, the other thing besides raising my boys. And then my 6-year-old fell in love with reading and took books everywhere—to the park, to school, to church, to bed. In the five minutes it took his brother to get out of the car, he would read two pages. I realized I could do that, too.

So in the margins—waiting in the pickup line at school, for the twenty minutes they played outside and I prepared dinner, in the fifteen minutes of silent reading time before naps started—I opened up a writing notebook and taught myself to write in short bursts.

3. There is no possession worth more than a relationship.

I still remember the conversation I had with Husband when our first son was born.

"We'll teach him not to touch all the pretty things on our tables so he won't do it when he goes to other people's houses."

I would laugh at that couple today.

Just after my second son was born, there came a sleep-deprived morning when my oldest, 2 at the time, found a glass ball sitting on a table. It was new, a gift from a new friend. He thought it was a ball, because that's exactly what it looked like, so he threw it. It shattered all over the tile floor.

I let out a long, piercing scream. I didn't even scream at him, just screamed, and Husband, who was napping at the time, came flying down the stairs to see what was wrong. He took in the mess on the floor and my crying toddler and his crying wife, and he said, "I think you may need sleep more than I do. Go rest."

I did, but as I was leaving, I heard my 2-year-old say, "Mama is mad at me."

We put away all the stuff that mattered that day, because my relationship with my sons is much more important than a meaningless glass ball.

Later, when I accidentally broke one of his crayons, my son said, "That's okay. I know it was just an accident."

4. Fun can be found anywhere.

Out back they find sticks and sword fight, or they play trampoline dodgeball or they stand under the umbrella out on the back deck and pretend like it's raining hard enough to melt them into a little puddle of lava. They make science projects by freezing toys in water, timing how long it takes to defrost them.

They don't need a whole house of toys or expensive trips around the country to have a good time. All they really need is a few sticks and an old sheet for a teepee, or a box they can carve into an astronaut helmet, or a couple of blue blankets to turn the couch into an ocean. Their imagination is limitless.

5. Tomorrow is always a brand new day.

No matter how many times I fail at keeping calm when my children misbehave, I have learned that there is always an opportunity to start over again. Children have the most forgiving hearts, if we are willing to apologize to them for losing our cool. They have the most forgetting hearts, too—which can seem like starting completely over every single day—so not only do they forgive when we are not our best selves, but they also willingly forget. They are more than willing to re-establish our connection as parent and child and move on.

I'd like to be more like my children.

I want to let them teach me. I want to learn from their imaginations, and I want to love like they do, and I want to see the whole glorious world with their eyes.

I'll teach them much along their way, of course. But I wonder sometimes who the greater teacher will be. I suspect it will probably be the six boys crammed inside my house, destroying my bathrooms, rearranging my heart.

What to Do With the Question, 'Were You Trying for a Girl?'

I have a lot of kids. That's true any way you slice it up. I have a lot of kids, and I have a lot of boys.

Invariably, when we are out and about as a family, someone will take a look at all these kids who are all boys and stride over to us for one single purpose: to ask the question that burns in the minds of the most curious people.

"Are these all yours?" they'll say.

We'll laugh. Yes, we'll say. These are all ours.

At this point, the conversation can take a number of turns—some of them more fun and entertaining than others. But one of my least favorites is when people reach for the next words they can think to say and those words happen to be: "You were trying for a girl, weren't you."

Sometimes people are only asking as a joke or out of curiosity. Sometimes they're asking with derision decorating their question. I can always tell the difference. But it doesn't matter with what intent they ask, this question always raises my defenses a little.

Husband and I will look at our wonderful boys and back at the well meaning person—we know they don't always know what to say. We get that. It's hard to know what to say to someone who's made a different choice than you have, and we are quite the spectacle when we are out on the town. We realize all of this, and we try to be gentle and loving in our responses. But we'll look them straight in the eye and we'll say, "We were given six boys, and we're happy about it."

And our boys, who are always listening, will smile and go on playing.

Here's the thing. Well meant questions are not always innocent, even if we intend them to be. I learned this back when my oldest was only five, and he said to me on the way to school one day, "If one of us died, you wouldn't be that sad, would you?"

I was shocked by this question.

"What do you mean, baby?" I said. "Of course I would be sad. I'd be so very sad if I lost one of my boys."

"But you said you only wanted four, and now you have five," he said.

The whole world shifted under my feet. I felt unsteady for a moment. I remembered something that I had said as a joke, when another well meaning person had asked the very question that I've referenced above. I had just had my twin boys, and we had gone out for our first shopping trip with all of my children—a 5-year-old, a 2-year-old, a 1-year-old, and newborn twins. Husband was with me, for support purposes. Someone fawned over our twins, which was usual in the beginning, and then she stepped back from us and said, "You were trying for a girl, weren't you."

Husband and I, weary from lack of sleep and ready to be home in a place where we could relax a bit, laughed a little, and I said, "Well, you know, we thought we'd try one more time, and then we got twins."

My 5-year-old had interpreted this to mean that his daddy and I only wanted four children, and because we got five, we must not have wanted one of them.

So you can see how the question above might damage a boy who is listening. And boys are always listening. I don't want them to ever think that one of them was unwanted because I longed for a girl. And of course I longed for a girl. Doesn't every mother long for a daughter? But every mother also takes what she has been given and loves that child wholeheartedly, regardless of gender.

Now I have six boys. I have been able to tell my oldest son, who is 9, that his daddy and I CHOSE to have six. There is no doubt in his mind that they were all wanted. We did our own family planning, and this is the family we were given. I love this family.

But the comments have not ceased. People get quite creative in the way they ask or declare, "Are you going to try for a girl one more time?" "You were just trying for a girl and you got another boy." "You really should try again."

As if I am not perfectly and completely satisfied with my tribe of boys. As if I am lacking something.

I lack nothing.

My boys are amazing little people. They are strong, courageous, kind, and they love their mama in a fiercely beautiful way. I wouldn't have traded any one of them for a daughter.

I used to discourage my boys from answering when people asked their daddy or me if we were trying for a girl. But I let them answer now. And they tell these well meaning people that they *did* have a sister. She died. And this is true. I am the mother of a daughter. I never got to hold her, but I am still her mother.

I know full well that most of the comments we get are completely innocent and all in jest. People don't really mean any harm, and even if they do, I prefer to believe they don't. The problem is that my boys are always listening, so I have to reframe these curiosities. I have to make sure that my sons always feel valued and know that they were welcome additions to our family, not means to another end—an end we never got to see.

I don't want my boys to ever apologize for being boys because they think their mama would have been happier with a daughter.

The thing about wanting something—like a daughter—is that we don't always know what we really need when we're blinded by what we want. I needed boys so that I could become more comfortable with myself and who I am and what my body looks like. I needed boys so that I could give up my high expectations of a perfectly tidy, perfectly clean house. I needed boys so I could loosen up, have a little fun, be a little rowdy and gross if I wanted.

And let me tell you, I have perfected my childhood dreams of becoming the Best Burper at the Table. Which is perfectly all right with me.

Dear Firstborn Son: You Were the First

"I'm halfway to being an adult," you said just this morning, and I nearly collapsed with the grief of it, because it feels like just yesterday, because you are my precious boy, because you were the first. And you saw. Your face changed completely, and you followed it up with, "It's okay. I'll take my time."

But you won't, my boy, because it's what all children do: long to be adults, and I will watch the next nine years fly by just as fast as these last nine have, and then you will be grown and gone. There is an exhilaration and a sadness to this, as there is to every stage of child-raising. But especially with the child who first wrapped a tiny cry around our hearts.

Because you know what? It was not just you who were born nine years ago. It was me, too. You and I, we share a birthday—yours a coming into the world, mine a coming into a whole new world made more alive and colorful and lovely because of you.

I know it's not easy being the first. You were, after all, our grand experiment. Your daddy and I had no idea what we were doing when you slid into the world, and sometimes we still don't. You are heart and spirit and muscle and feet and sun and tornado, ripping away everything we thought we knew about how to do this raising-a-child thing and planting yourself right in the middle of a wilderness that would test us and beat us and tear us apart but, in the end, put us back together with all the right pieces, like a puzzle we'd forgotten we had until you let loose your wild wind and uncovered all the years. It's you who has shown us the right boundaries to set, and it's you who has shown us what it means to love a child, and it's you who has shown us more surely who we are.

That's not to say that your brothers haven't. It's just that you were the first. The first one I laid in a crib and worried about all night until I couldn't stand it anymore and went out to watch you breathing. The first one whose smile climbed down to the deepest places and said, "Adored," so loud I could believe it. The first one who one minute made me feel so incredibly glad to be your mom and the next minute made me feel so angry I thought I'd burn right up in flames and smoke and haze.

You tested boundaries to see if they held strong. You shook the foundations of our philosophies. You let loose your whirlwind, and we were caught in chaos and fear, but mostly adoration and love. Because you were remaking us, piece by piece, limb by limb, in all the ways that mattered. So it is that we have learned how to navigate stormy waters of doubt and hope. So it is that we have learned to pry our hands loose from what happens in all the can't-be-there places of your life. So it is that we have learned to parent in a way that feels and understands and loves in all the littlest ways.

We have made some mistakes. Of course we have. For those, we're sorry.

But there is one, my sweet boy, that I cannot just slap a sorry on. Because I think it deserves more. So bear with me.

I spent my pregnancy with you laughing about your spirited kicks while sifting through parenting books so I might be at least a little bit prepared, maybe, for what was to come. Still, your daddy and I started out as authoritarians, because that's how we were raised. It's all we knew. When you know better, you do better, but we wouldn't know better until four years later. So, for the meantime, we ignored emotions and hit while we told you not to hit and yelled while we told you not to yell. Do better than we do, that's what we said in our actions. Be better than us. Choose the higher road, and you were just a boy.

How could a heart not be traumatized by inconsistencies like that?

And then I opened a Paul Eckert book on reading emotions in the eyes, and I saw your eyes on the page. They were darker than yours and smaller, with bushier eyebrows. But they were yours. Do you know what the caption said? Despair.

A little boy in a little body, crying out for help. Crying out for understanding. Crying out for someone to fight for his heart and help him back to a steady plane, because he was in danger of losing his step and his breath and who he was made to be.

I still remember that day. I don't want to. But I need to. Because that was the day I fell to my knees and said, for the first time, "We need a better way." That was the day that launched us into years of study, years of research, years of grasping for something that was right and true and good, and we found it. And even though we weren't perfect at it, you no longer wore those despair eyes. Sometimes you wore angry eyes, when you had to put away a drawing pad and you weren't quite ready to. Sometimes you wore sad eyes, when the book was supposed to be waiting on the hold shelf of the library and it wasn't there. But mostly you wore happy ones.

We talked more. We accepted all the emotions, not just the convenient ones. We held your body when it flew out of control, whispering the only words you really need to hear: *This is hard. I am here. You are safe.*

And now here we are. Your ninth birthday. You are leaning closer to young man than little boy now, and I am so proud of and enthralled with and captivated by who you are. I am still just as wrecked by your eyes and your smile and your voice as I was the day you slipped into the world five days early, smelling of eucalyptus and mint, because that's the lotion that softened my hands and touched every part of your silken face. You are my beloved one. My spirited one. My firstborn son.

You are deeply and wholly loved, just because you're you.

Dear Last-Born Son: These Things You Should Know

It takes only a look from those evening sky eyes, so much like your daddy's, before I'm lost in time, lost in space, lost in a world where only you and I exist. It takes only one sweet, joyful smile to send me reeling, end over end, in a twister of tears, for the growing up and the getting older and the never again. It takes only one slobbery kiss to crawl all the way down to my depths and remind me, *This is it.*

This is it. You are it. You are the last born son.

We knew it from the first moment we knew of you. You grew and you kicked and you formed so perfectly, so beautifully, so wonderfully, and I tried to enjoy every minute of your growing, before I'd even met you, because this was the last time.

It's funny how a new baby comes into a family by storm, how those first few months feel blurry and unreal, and then, looking back, it's hard to remember a time when new baby was no baby. I try to see what life was like before you, and it's impossible to remember what I did with my nights but give you the last goodnight, sleep tight kiss. It's impossible to remember what I did with my mornings but burrow my face into your belly to make you laugh. It's impossible to remember afternoons without your curled-up form, sleeping soundly in a crib or my arms.

Ours is not a complete family without you.

I know your brothers would agree. You are the light of their day, smiling no matter how the world is falling apart around you, calling to them when they pass you on their way to the refrigerator, missing them when they're away at school. You are sunshine in a hurricane. You are morning song splitting a silent night. You are breath and hope and life and love and miracle.

I spent my birthday last year holding you, just three hours old, against my chest, and I did not think that I would ever put you down, because you were beautiful, and you were here and you were ALIVE and you were last.

And then we brought you home and you fit right in like the whole world had waited on you before it started turning again, in just the right way. Your brothers lived for one little smile, one little contagious laugh, one little hand pat on their leg. You looked around for them when they were gone, because the noise was a constant in your existence, and you did not know, exactly, what to do without it.

It's hard to explain what you mean to me. But I will try.

That first moment in the hospital, you looked into my eyes, and you reminded me that I mattered. You were born on the day before my birthday, and I'd always had a complicated relationship with birthdays, because there was always someone missing from mine, but you reminded me that my birthday mattered, that I mattered. You have no idea what that did for me, my sweet. I was able to unfold in your first year of life in ways I had never done. I was able to dream truer and hope wider. I was able to, finally, live.

You are my last-born son. You are the culmination of eight years of childbearing, a whole lifetime of longing. I have given my skin, my eyes, my nose, my mouth, my hair to all of you, some getting more of one than others. Mostly, though, I have given my heart, marveling at who you are and how beautiful this mothering is and what a wonder it is that you are all here, breathing, sleeping, living out loud in the very center of me.

But, you see, there is a sadness you brought with you. If, in the future, you happen to notice this sadness splitting my face, you must know that it is nothing to do with you and everything to do with you. Because everything I watch you do will be the last time.

Your first smile—it was the last first smile I would see from one of my babies. Your first wobbling steps—those were the last first steps I'll ever see from my own. That 2 a.m. feeding, the sweet silence of it, was the last 2 a.m. feeding I will experience.

A slight sadness slides in with the last child, but I want you to know, today and always, that it has nothing to do with who you are. You will see the sadness in my face the first day of kindergarten, but it has nothing to do with who you are. You will see the sadness in my smile when you walk the stage at your fifth-grade graduation ceremony, but it has nothing to do with how you've done or who you've grown to be. You will see the sadness in my pride the day you drive away from home, but it has nothing to do with who you have been beneath our roof.

You will be the last one who learns to drive a car and the last one who takes Algebra II and the last one who marches in the school band or sings in the choir or lines up on a football field. You will be the last one to go to the senior prom, and you will be the last one to pack your stuff and leave home. And so all along this growing up will be moments of such great pride and wonder, and they will be moments of profound grief and pain, too.

Soon, you will learn to wield a spoon, and you will learn to dress yourself, and you will learn to tie your own shoes, and there is a grief in this passing away, because what does a mother do when she has nothing left to do? When she is not needed for the day-to-day functioning anymore? When she is just an important person in a life instead of a vital, I-can't-make-it-without-her person?

Well, she loves. She keeps on loving. She keeps on.

I know we're a long way from those days of doing for yourself and walking to school on your own and leaving home for good, but here we are, in the blink of an eye, at your first birthday, and it's the last first birthday I'll experience with a child of my own. So it is a day of celebration, and it is a day of sadness.

This evening I will pack away your clothes, which you outgrew weeks ago but which I've been slow to clear out, because *it's the last time*. I will mail them to your cousin, and, meanwhile, you will keep growing up, never to stop, no matter how desperately I want you to stop, for just a small moment in time so I can preserve that gummy smile and commit it to memory forever and ever and ever, so I can remember the way you reach for me every time I come into a room because I'm your favorite person in the world, so I can watch you giggle and laugh and do a dance of your own when your brothers turn the music too loud. I don't want the moments to go away, and, like every moment, they must.

So I guess what I want you to know on your birthday is this: You are perfect just the way you are. I love you with all the love I have in my heart. You are a wondrous ending point to our family with your great joy and wide smile and sweet nature.

Happy birthday, my love. You are mine for now.

What Kid-Picked Flowers Can Teach Mothers About Beauty

It never fails. We're out walking our boys to school, or we're taking a spirited romp through nature, or I'm just sitting inside working on something, and a boy will barge through my door and hand me a wildflower he picked.

My boys get pretty passionate about this quest. Just this morning, on the way to school, the 5-year-old socked his 3-year-old brother, because he'd picked a flower for me and accidentally dropped it, and the 3-year-old stomped on it on purpose. The 5-year-old got angry, because he was going to give that flower to Mama, and now it was ruined. This was cause for revenge.

The other day, when I was standing at my computer working, the 5-year-old burst through my door with a whole bouquet of wildflowers. The spring here in Texas has been rainy and warm, and the wildflowers have been growing faster than we can mow them down in our yard, but thankfully the homeowners association hasn't been complaining about it. At least not yet. My boys, however, do a grand enough job of picking these wildflowers and gathering them for me. This particular day had been a rough day, and the 5-year-old brought that bouquet up and had tied it all together with a bit of string, and he laid it on my desk without saying much of anything. He smiled when I caught his eye. I told him thank you, the emotion clogging my throat, and he hugged me.

My desk could do with a little prettying, and it was the perfect gift for me. It's still sitting over there, even though the flowers have long since dried up.

My boys see flowers on the side of the street, and they can't help but pick them and thrust them at me. "Put them in your hair, Mama," they'll say, and I'll have to thread them through my strands pulled back in a ponytail. They'll pick some on the way to school and give them to their teacher. They'll hand them out to random women and girls on their walk.

When I've asked them why, they nearly always have the same answer. "Because you're beautiful," they say.

And every woman they meet is beautiful, too. They all deserve flowers.

I love this sentiment. I love that they have such generous hearts. I love that they look at a woman and they see beauty, regardless of who the woman is or what she looks like. Kids have such forgiving lenses.

I don't always see myself as beautiful. This struggle has become easier as a mother—but it is not, by any means, solved. There are many days that I see myself as the one stem in a field of wildflowers that didn't actually bloom. There are many days when I wish I could be different, like that other mother who doesn't carry as much baby weight or the one who actually tries to look her best every day or the one who is confident enough to show some skin—something I've never been confident doing.

I forget that we are all different, and we are meant to be. There is not a flower that is exactly like another. We have different numbers of petals, we have different ways of blooming, we have different bends to our stems.

When my 5-year-old brought that bouquet of flowers, I thought long and hard about how my boys see those beautiful flowers in a field and immediately think of me, because they see me through the lens of love and not the lens of what society says I, as a woman and a mother, should be. They don't see me as needing to change or reinvent myself at all. They aren't aware of the ways I don't measure up, the ways I don't fit the perfect definition of beauty, the ways I am not good enough. They only see me as Mama. They only see me as beautiful.

I want to receive that.

So now, every time I walk down the street to their school and one of them hands me a wildflower, yellow or purple or pink, to put in my hair, I do it, but not before I think about how this flower, as beautiful as it is, brought me to the mind of my boys. I think about how my beauty is much more than what I look like on the outside—it is my strength, my courage, my patience, my hard work and determination, my dedication, my sacrificial commitment, my creativity, my love. It is who I am.

Who I am is beautiful.

The Surprising Disadvantages of Potty Training

The 4-year-old races to the bathroom, and I hear him call through the open door. "Is anyone coming over, Mama?"

"No," I say. "Why?"

He peers out of the bathroom door, his brown-black eyes crinkling a little at the corners. "Because I peed a little in my underwear. So I can't put them back on."

And then he races out of the bathroom completely naked and wraps a blanket around himself and resumes putting together his robot puzzle on the dining room table.

Even though there are days like today, I still have to say it out loud: I have successfully potty trained five boys.

It bears repeating, doesn't it? I have successfully potty trained five boys.

This feels like it may be one of the most significant achievements of a lifetime. Forget writing and publishing books. Forget producing musical albums. Forget all those awards and accolades.

I HAVE SUCCESSFULLY POTTY TRAINED FIVE BOYS.

Most days, I am glad for this. Sincerely. Diapers get old fast, and once these boys hit 2 years old and those diapers moved up a whole level from stinking into reeking, I said it was time.

But then there are days like today, when I walk into the bathroom with only my socks and step on a pair of wet underwear a boy slipped off when he waited too long to take care of business, because he just wants to play.

There are days when a boy will let me know he accidentally wet the bed this morning fifteen minutes before it's time to get in bed for the night and that boy will now have to sleep without a waterproof cover or a sheet or a blanket, just stretched out on a mattress.

There are days when the just-got-potty-trained 2-year-old will think his carpet looks like the right place to pee, instead of the potty that's a mere twenty steps away from his doorway.

There are days when a 4-year-old will forget how badly he needs to go, and he will do his favorite trick—the handstand—and the pee that just couldn't wait will spray all over his face and hair in the most remarkably amazing way.

There are days when the two 2-year-olds will forget to potty before they get into a warm bath, and they spray each other in the eye before they even know what's happening.

There are days when we wake up and visit the boys' bathroom and find pee all over the seat and the floor because a little boy wasn't so good at aiming when he was half asleep.

There are days when a wall gets soaked with a urine-stream, because a boy was peeing and a brother came in the bathroom with an amazing LEGO creation, and the peeing boy couldn't help but turn and admire it.

There are days when boys will climb to the top of a van and wonder what it would be like to drop their drawers and pee from the top of it, with all the neighbors watching, so the pee waters the plants all around, and, also, the van windows, which were in desperate need of a washing.

There are days when boys get back from trick-or-treating and they're examining their treats on the floor of the living room and Iron Man will pee right through his costume, because looking at his candy is way more fascinating and exciting than visiting the bathroom, and his brothers will cry out, "The candy! Move the candy!"

There are days when a board game is spread out on the kitchen table and one little boy, who can't really see the table when he's sitting, will stand up, and because he's thinking way more deeply about his next move than he's thinking about how he needs to go to the potty, he will pee all over those board game pieces.

There are days when I will pick up their blanket to put back on their bed, and it will smell like it was soaked in a pee pond.

There are days when the 5-year-old forgets to potty before he gets in the bath, and he will stand on the lip of the bathtub and try to aim his pee into the foot-away toilet, and he will miss all over yours truly.

So much pee everywhere in our house.

Sometimes there are days when I think maybe diapers weren't so bad after all.

I know that one day they'll be masters at this, too. I know they won't forever leave their territory marks all over the house.

Until then, I guess I'll just have to get used to the house smelling like a swamp. At least it doesn't smell like a sweaty locker room. Yet.

I Did Not Even Try to Breastfeed My Last Son

I did not even try to breastfeed my youngest son.

When I go out to the store to pick up the can of formula that has fed and grown him these last five weeks, I almost always go to the checkout line where a man is working—because I know how it will go if it's a woman ringing up my can of formula.

She will look at me, and she will look at the tiny baby in the infant seat at the front of my grocery cart, and then she will look back at me, and her eyes will grow just the slightest shade darker, and she won't know it, but I will see the way her lips press together when she asks that question, "Find everything you needed?"

She will, in her subtle way, communicate that she does not think I'm a good mother.

I know, because I have been through this five times before.

I know, because five of my children have been raised on formula.

I know, because, in our society, a woman who does not try to breastfeed her baby is not a good mother, or at least that's the story we like to tell.

The problem is, I did try.

This is what those women who eye me like I should not be able to take my precious baby home don't know about me. This is what you cannot see when you observe a mother buying formula for her newborn baby.

When my first boy slid into the world eight years ago, I had every intention of breastfeeding. I notified the nurses and kept him by my side, because I knew nursing frequently would increase my milk supply, and I did everything I was told by the lactation consultant who visits with every new mother while she's trapped in a hospital. His latch was good, he was feeding well, I was all set.

And then they released me, and I went home, and two days later we brought him right back to the hospital for dehydration, because he hadn't produced a wet diaper in twelve hours, and I wasn't willing to supplement, because breast is best.

I watched them stick my four-day-old with IVs that kept popping out, because his veins were too small—one in his foot, one in his wrist, and then, finally, one in the side of his head.

I sobbed and he screamed and we spent six hours waiting for him to hydrate, hoping we'd be able to take him home for the Thanksgiving dinner set to happen at our house in less than twelve hours.

Nurses sent us home with liquid formula. I cried pouring it into a bottle. I cried calling the lactation consultant and setting up the second meeting. I cried on the drive over.

The lactation consultant watched me breastfeed. She watched me pump. She gave me a device I could fill with formula and attach a tiny straw to my breast so he would still have to work to get his milk, instead of getting it easily from a bottle. She told me to feed, pump, feed, pump, feed, pump.

I did everything I was told, lined up those water bottles so I could make sure I was adequately hydrated. I fed him every hour and pumped on the half hour, never getting more than a quarter of an ounce, most times less than that.

I was up all night and all day. And then, after six weeks of too little sleep and too much crying and too much stinging disappointment, I quit.

I quit because it didn't work, because I'd done my best, because I just wanted to enjoy my baby.

The same happened with my second boy, minus the hospital stay, because I knew what to look for. I quit after five weeks.

Same with the third. I quit after four weeks.

And then there were twins. I knew if I couldn't produce enough milk for one baby, I couldn't produce enough for two, but I tried anyway. I quit after a week.

So now, here I am, with my sixth and last baby. I did not even try to breastfeed him. And even though I know my story, when we're out in public, I hide the formula canister, because I know what happens and what people assume about mothers like me.

Some of us didn't choose not to breastfeed. We just couldn't.

It's a painful thing, to know that you are supposed to be able to feed and nourish your baby but you can't. I wanted that bonding time. I wanted to say, like my friends, that every pound he gained was gained because of my amazing body. I wanted my babies to be smart and healthy and close to me.

I surely didn't want to be broken.

But my boys have grown into some of the smartest kids you'll ever meet. I can count on one hand the number of times they've been sick (and there are six of them!). They love their mama in extravagant ways.

Even though I sometimes feel the familiar ache at not being able to fully nourish my last son, I know that he will grow in the same way his brothers have before him—and, more importantly, I know that I truly enjoyed the first weeks of his life, without pressure.

Sometimes breast isn't best.

The Miraculous Gift of a Son on a Birthday

I am holding him in my arms, and I can't stop staring, because he is so beautiful and so miraculous and so peaceful, and he is my last.

That he slid into the world on the day before my birthday feels like a great, significant gift. I did not care that I was recovering in a hospital bed on the day my mother welcomed me into the world, because he was here, and he was safe, and he was most wonderfully alive.

There were days, weeks, months, when we did not know if that would be so.

There came a day, just past my thirty-fourth week of pregnancy, when I began to itch, uncomfortably so. I don't remember it starting in my hands and feet, which is where it typically starts, I just remember lying in bed and feeling like I needed to scratch out my eyes for a little bit of relief.

I casually mentioned it in conversation with my doctor, still thinking that maybe I'd gotten into something I was allergic to, but her face changed a little—only slightly, because she's delivered all my babies and knows my penchant for anxiety. She ordered blood tests, and I tried not to look it up on Mayo clinic, but, of course, I did. But Husband took away my phone when he saw what I was doing, so I didn't even get to see how I was dying this time.

Blood tests confirmed that I had an incredibly rare pregnancy condition—cholestasis of the liver.

I came home, and because Husband wasn't around to take my phone away, I looked up everything I could about it. All those articles pointed to one serious thing: a high risk of stillbirth.

I freaked. My doctor told me to do kick counts, which I did, religiously, crying my way through them, because what if I did a kick count and let my guard down and then suddenly the kicks stopped coming? I talked to my baby, every minute I could, because what if I didn't get to meet him? I breathed through all the panic attacks when he stopped moving for five minutes and I noticed.

I begged my doctor to deliver, every time I went into her office.

I guess I wore her down, because three weeks before his due date, she started the pitocin drip, hooked up the baby heart monitor, and we all waited.

He slid out perfectly perfect and alive.

They put him in my arms, still sticky, and I could not stop kissing his sweet little face, because here was a baby, alive, on the evening before my birthday, and I don't think there is any greater gift than new life.

Since that day, I have not been able to put him down, this love-gift on a birthday.

That he is my last, that he was given so close to my special day, that he is alive, sleeping in my arms and tearing open my heart every minute of every day, like his brothers did before him, is beautiful and miraculous and wonderful, and I will never be the same.

My family will never be the same.

There are days when it feels like my boys are weighing me down physically and emotionally, but this boy, this last son, is a message—

a reminder—that they are all precious gifts.

    So I will carry him in my arms and hold him while he sleeps and kiss his sweet face a million times a day.

    Because he is a last gift.

    And he is mine for now.

How to Answer the Question, 'You're Done, Right?'

We're walking downtown, on our way to a park close to the city's center, because one of my boys has a birthday and has asked to come here. We're just about to cross the road when a high-pitched laugh sounds behind us.

"Oh, my God," a woman says, loudly enough so all of us waiting at the corner for the crosswalk signal to turn green can hear her. At first I think she couldn't possibly be talking to us, and then she says, "Six BOYS? These are all yours?"

She looks from Husband to me and then back again. Husband smiles politely at her, uncomfortable at her forthcoming and obnoxiously loud observation. She stares at us, still waiting for an answer.

"Yes," I say. "They're all ours." There are twins strapped in a stroller and a newborn strapped to me and the older boys gripping the sides of the stroller. I look at them all and can almost sympathize with her. We make quite a spectacle, truth be told.

"You're done, right?" she says.

Husband and I laugh good-naturedly, but inside I'm seething. It's not your business, I want to say. Rude, I want to say. As if we owe you any explanation, I want to say. But I don't, because I'm a nice person, and, thankfully, the crosswalk dings and it's time to be on our way. She quickly leaves us behind, because it takes eight people longer to cross a street in one piece. But her words hang behind, with us. And then, as if she can sense that her words are still with us, she turns around again.

"I bet you're busy," she says.

Yes, we are. It's a wild and crazy house.

"But, seriously, you're done, right?" She's walking, but she folds her arms across her chest. My boys look from her to their daddy and then to me. They don't really know what we're talking about, but they do know a lot about emotions, and since I'm afraid they might be able to see what I think on my face, I smile sweetly at her again and laugh, hoping she'll go on her nosy way.

Earlier this day, we walked our kids past the San Antonio Alamo, where the city's annual Fiesta activities were in full swing. We always elicit stares, but most people are courteous enough to give us the space we need to execute an outing like this one. Some of them even help if one of the kids gets separated from us, and I'm always grateful to those kind, protective souls, glad I live in a city where people look out for each other.

An hour before this woman sauntered up behind us to comment on the state of our reproductive choices, we'd stopped at the downtown mall, because we'd left our picnic lunch on the dining room table at home, and, of course, the kids were hungry. We bought them a snack, and during the forty-five minutes we trapped them at a table, three women stopped by our table to tell me how beautiful and well behaved my boys are. Not one of these women asked me if we were done yet, because they recognize the value of a family like mine.

There are times when people tell me they love to see our family out and about, creating beauty in the world, and they wish, more than anything, that they had decided to have more children.

And then there are times like this.

We are a larger-than-average family living in a society that likes to point out that the world is way too overpopulated and that it is irresponsible to have so many children and that we are crazy to pretend we enjoy having a large family with so many children. I know. I've read their comments on my essays and seen their hate mail in my inbox.

But what they don't really know or understand is that crazy people like me actually enjoy having a large family. As annoying as it can get sometimes when all they've been doing all day is having a slap-fight and I want to join them, I can't imagine a single one of them gone from my life. Sure, life would be easier and less complicated if I didn't have six kids to usher into the car when we're on our way anywhere. Sure, I'd have more time alone if there weren't six of them vying for my attention. Sure, I might not have as many gray hairs if I'd only had one or two.

But the fact is, my family is awesome. We're going to change the world together.

So I'm just going to assume that everyone who wants to comment on my large family is agreeing with me. It's a much better way to live anyway.

Next time someone asks me if I'm done, I'll turn to them, look them in the eye, and say one of two responses: "Done with what?" or "Not until I get my own reality TV show."

Because humor covers a multitude.

3 Harmless Lies I Tell My Children

The other day I was warming up the leftovers I had from the very rare night out with Husband. My boys are like vultures. They can smell food—especially restaurant food—from ten miles away.

"What's that smell?" the 4-year-old said.

"My lunch," I said, stressing the word *my*.

He peeked into the toaster oven, where it was warming up. "Oooh," he said, looking up at me with those big brown doe-eyes that are so very hard to resist. "That looks yummy."

I knew what he was waiting for, but I was not about to offer him a bite of my fish and chips, because if I offer a bite to one, there are four others who will come begging, even if they're outside where no food smell has currently reached them. My boys intuitively know when one gets something the other doesn't.

When I didn't offer a bite, he said, "Can I have some?"

"No," I said.

"Why not?"

"This is adult food," I said. "It will make you sick."

He didn't argue, just looked incredibly disappointed.

This is only one of the lies I tell my children. I don't tell it often, only when they're wondering why that kid sitting across his lunchroom gets to have a cupcake with his McDonalds lunch and all we've got is pineapple and kiwi for dessert. There's a simple answer to that: It will make you sick—which is not entirely untrue.

When they want to know why all their friends get to watch television once they get home from school but they, my sons, have to do art or build with LEGO pieces or go outside or write in their mandatory journals or read a book, the answer is, "Because it will make your brain sick." Which is also not entirely untrue. When they ask why they can't have their tenth taco in one sitting, that's easy. "Because it will make you sick." This may or may not be true.

Another lie I often tell my children is "I don't know." This one often pops up when they've been talking SO MUCH for SO LONG, asking all these questions that I answer patiently until the five hundredth one sends me careening off the cliffs of insanity. This usually happens when I'm trying to figure out where I put the carrot peeler and the chicken noodle soup is boiling over on the stove and someone comes to see what's happening in the kitchen, asking, "What are we having for dinner?"

"I don't know," I'll say.

"But you're cooking it," he'll say.

Really, "I don't know" is just code for "please don't talk to me right now, I'm trying to fix dinner and I'm concentrating and I don't know where I put the carrot peeler or whether I already salted the broth or why I could possibly have forgotten the noodles when I went to the store for ingredients." In this situation.

Legitimately, there are things that I don't know, so this isn't always a lie. When kids ask me how many teeth a shark has, for instance, I don't know. When they ask me why farts smell, I don't know (but I'll look it up for cheap entertainment). When they ask me to name all the ninety-five Power Buddies they made up as characters to make sure I was listening when they listed them all (I wasn't), I don't know.

But there are other things I do know. Like when they ask me when their birthday is for the ten thousandth time, or when they ask me to build them a robot out of LEGOs for the thirtieth time this second because theirs broke again, or when they ask me to fix the wheel on the helicopter that has been in the donation pile fifty times already and somehow keeps reappearing or when they ask me how to spell "wrong" and I've been telling them for the last hour how to spell all the words they want to use in an inappropriately long letter from a 4-year-old to his Nonny.

"I don't know" can be convenient every now and then.

And then there's the "that's probably why it happened" lie. I use this when one of my twins has just grabbed a train away from his brother and, while he's running away, he slams into a wall, because he was not paying attention to what was in front of him, only the angry brother chasing behind. I use this sometimes when a boy is tripping his brothers on the trampoline and then he jumps off and his leg gets caught in the rope ladder and he's stuck hanging upside down, yelling, "Help!" I use it every time one of the boys threatens to change the Amazon music station, because he doesn't like the one I chose, and on his way to do what he was strictly forbidden not to do, he trips over his own shoe, which he kicked off as soon as he got home, and gives himself a bloody lip.

After consoling the hurt boy, I'll sneak it in there. "It probably happened because you were trying to do something we told you not to do."

It's not my finest parenting hour, but there is a bit of satisfaction we feel when the one who is dancing all over our last nerve gets what's coming to him. That's human nature. Becoming a mother didn't elevate me out of humanity's depravity, apparently.

Unfortunately, I've found these lies sneaking into other areas of my life. When Husband said he was going to have one more cookie and I was counting on that last cookie being mine, the first thing that came to mind is "It will make you sick." When my mother called to talk and got to the point in the conversation where she asks about what my kids are doing, I didn't want to complain anymore, so I said, "I don't know." When Husband told me about how an old bully of a coworker got fired, I said, "That's probably why it happened."

I know that, eventually, my kids will figure out that these words are not strictly true, and I don't want them to believe that every wrong action will give them a bloody lip or hang them upside down from a rope ladder or that they'll be punished in any way for their wrong actions, because I'm not that kind of parent. But every now and then, these lies come in handy.

My third son just found my dark chocolate stash. Looks like it's time to pull out "It'll make you sick."

Do Parents Have a Favorite Child? Of Course

I have a favorite child today.

It's the boy who carried my laptop down the stairs because his mama's foot is broken and he knows she needs a free hand to hold onto the stair rail so she doesn't fall again. He carries it so carefully his eyes are opened wide in concentration, and he places it exactly in the right place on the couch where he knows I always sit at this time to feed the baby.

He's my favorite until it's nap time and he won't put away the LEGO pieces he wanted to play with and then, when my back is turned because I'm putting the littlest one down, he smuggles that (quite impressive) creation under the covers and thinks I can't hear him snapping and unsnapping pieces.

Then my favorite is the one who stacks his books into a neat little pile at the foot of his bed instead of scattered all over the floor like a book carpet, who fell asleep right away and didn't need any reminders that right now is nap time and not play time.

He's my favorite until he decides to wake all his napping brothers, because he fell asleep first—which means he's logically the first one awake again—and he looks at the hangers in his closet and thinks they might be a perfect tool to use in his wake-up plan, so he craftily removes all the clothing from the hangers, arranging shirts and pants and even shoes in what looks like crime scene positions all over the floor and then rains the hangers all over the faces of his sleeping brothers.

Then my favorite is the one who remembers to go potty before we get in the car to go pick up his older brothers from school and isn't hysterically whining about how badly he needs to go potty and how he really, really, *really* doesn't want to go in his pants, which makes panic close off the back of my throat, because I really, really, *really* don't want to clean up a toddler's feces, but there's a school zone and kids running everywhere and no accessible bathroom that doesn't require unpacking everyone and at least fifteen minutes of wasted time, judging by the school pick-up line.

He's my favorite until we get back home and I'm helping his older brother put some things away and he decides he wants a cup instead of a thermos, even though, to date, he's only ever spilled a cup of anything and we've told him he needs to be a little bit older before he drinks from a lidless cup, and he does exactly what he nearly always does: spills it, and two boys slip in the water he didn't tell anyone was there.

Then my favorite is the boy who goes outside to play and comes back in with a wildflower he found in the yard that reminds him of me because it's so beautiful and he just had to pick it so I could put it in my hair and match beauty with beauty.

He's my favorite until he comes back downstairs in his third new outfit since he got home from school half an hour ago and proudly tells me he put both the previously worn shirts and shorts—worn for a collective ten minutes—in the dirty clothes hamper and not on his floor, and, also, he's wearing twelve pairs of socks.

Then my favorite is the one who lopes downstairs to ask if I want to listen to an audio book with him, because he knows I love reading while I'm cooking dinner and setting out plates, so I say, yes, of course, and we share a story while he sits at the table building LEGO creations and I brown some meat for tacos.

He's my favorite until he mentions casually over dinner that I might have thought he was doing homework in his room after school but what he was really doing was drawing his new comic book and he'll have to do his homework tomorrow morning (which will never happen. He and I both know this.).

When I was a kid, I was convinced that my mother had a favorite child. Now I understand that her favorite was always changing. Each one of my children can be my favorite in these snapshots of time when they do something or say something unexpectedly sweet or when they follow instructions to the letter or do what was asked without arguing or sassing.

Parents do have favorites. It's just that the favorite is always changing, constantly rotating through the inventory.

Except the baby, of course. He'll always be my favorite. At least until he hits age 3.

To My Kids: How to Survive When Mama is Away

I don't get many days off from children. Who am I kidding? The days-off count has been dialed to zero for the last several years.

But every now and then, my responsibilities as an author call me away for a night or two. When I'm called away, I celebrate—I mean, I miss them a ton. One thing I never do, though, is worry about Husband's capabilities as a parent.

Husband is a great father. He romps with his children and rubs courage into their chests every night and talks to them about their kid concerns and always has something wise and profound to say to them.

However. There are some things that even he has trouble with when I'm gone. I chalk it up to Being a Man. Things like turning off lights, flushing toilets, putting clothes in the laundry hamper, staying safe—they're all reasons why boys and men need a woman in their lives. I'm glad for that, mostly. Actually, no I'm not. Turn off the lights. Flush the toilets. Pick up your own clothes. And for God's sake, if you think something would be cool, don't try it. It's probably not, and you'll just end up with a cracked femur.

So for the days that I'm gone, I have a small stack of stapled papers, titled, "How to Survive When Mama is Away," populating a file folder that sits on our kitchen counter. The guide begins with "Dear Boys" and contains tips like:

1. This is how you turn out a light.

I know there seems to be a magic fairy who flies around flicking the light switches in all those empty rooms to the "off" position, but don't you worry. This isn't a hard trick, by any means. It just takes a little practice.

Do you see the white miniature lever surrounded by what looks like a white rectangle? That's called a light switch. When the lever is up, that means the light is on and our electricity meter is, minute by minute, climbing higher and the earth is slowly dying because of your negligence. When you leave a room and there is no one else in the room, the lever should move to the down position. That would be "off." If, on the other hand, you've just finished brushing your teeth and your little brother is still peeing, the lever should remain up, or "on." I know you sometimes get these two confused, and I totally understand. It's fun to hear, "Hey, turn the light back on!" But it's definitely not funny. Trust me. One of these days you'll get your due, and then you won't be laughing.

I'm sure that once you practice a little (and you'll have several opportunities, now that the magic fairy is gone for a couple of days), the muscle memory will kick in. After all, you used to turn lights off all the time when you were a baby. Up, down, up, down. On, off, on, off. You'll remember the joy you used to get out of actually making a room go dark when you weren't inside it.

And if you don't, there's an easy solution to that, too. Your allowance.

2. This is how you flush a toilet.

I appreciate that you want to save water and energy, but I can assure you that the environment will not be terribly harmed by a couple of flushes a day. The aroma of our house, on the other hand?

It could be called The Dead Swamp.

When you've done your business, stand up (if you're not standing already). Turn around to face the toilet (if you're not already facing it). Put the seat and, preferably, the lid down. On the left side, near the top of the porcelain, is a silver lever. That's the flusher. All you have to do is push it down. You don't even have to hold it down, just a quick flick and you're done. So easy.

And now no one has to lift the lid and find an unwelcome present that shoots stink bombs toward their nose.

3. This is where your dirty clothes go.

We have what is called a hamper for all of your dirty clothes. It's a tall, dark basket sitting in the hallway between your rooms. There's also a basket downstairs if you happen to strip down in the living room. And there's another in Mama and Daddy's bathroom. In it you'll likely only see Mama's clothes, but that's a conversation for another day.

The hamper is where your dirty laundry goes. Your dirty laundry does not belong in your closet. It does not belong in rolled-up wads under your bed. It does not belong in my bed, because if I wanted my pillow to smell like Dirty Sock, I would use my own stinky ones.

All you have to do to make sure clothes get in this thing called the hamper is bend over, pick your sweaty shirt up off the floor, and drop it in the hamper. You don't even have to walk anywhere, because you were so close when you threw it on the floor.

4. This is how you take a bath.

Unfortunately, while I'm gone, I won't be standing over you to make sure you soap up your hair and clean under your neck and wash between your toes. So this is how it's done: Take a squirt of soap and lather your hair. Take another squirt and lather it all over your body. Take another for your lower half. And another for your feet, because they need it.

Fill the cup sitting on the side of the bathtub with water and then dump it on your head to wash the soap out of your hair. Do it as many times as it takes to get all the soap off your body. It might take longer than you'd like, but, trust me, a few more minutes of rinsing is better than waking up in the morning looking like Donald Trump.

5. This is how you drain bath water.

I can't tell you how many times I have walked into your bathroom to see yesterday's murky bath water still stagnating in the tub. I usually stick my hand in that grainy, cloudy, slimy water, trying not to gag at the grossness, and drain it before it's time for your bath. I know this is probably why you think the water magically disappears, but I'm here to tell you that it doesn't really. And now that I'll be gone for a few days, it's a perfect opportunity for you to practice the Art of Draining Bathwater. There is a small amount of work required to successfully execute this task.

When you're finished washing (per my instructions), stand. Dry off BEFORE getting out of the bath, turn around, bend over, and pull the silver or bronze plug at the foot of the tub, directly underneath the faucet. Listen to the water slowly sucking out, and imagine something is coming up out of the drain to get you. Run away screaming.

(You don't have to do that last part.)

6. This is how you close a door.

Do you see the handle sticking out from the door? It's called a doorknob, and it's what you use to open the door. Funny thing is, you can also use it to close the door. Grab it on your way out and swing it the opposite way required for opening. It's easy to remember, because close is the opposite of open. So it stands to reason that to *close* a door, you'll have to use the opposite motion you used to open the door. Make sense?

The door will make a satisfying "click" when it's truly closed. Listen for the click, and you'll be well on your way to closing a door.

Other ways you can accomplish this same feat are using a hip bump when you walk in the door, aiming a back kick on your way out or executing a full-body lean in whichever direction you need. I don't really care what method you use, so long as it shuts.

Now that you know how to do all of these things, it's time for the most important one of all.

7. This is how not to die.

Do not jump from a swing when you've reached twenty feet in the air.

Do not climb on a glass-top table that's only held in place by (inefficiently spaced) suction cups.

Do not turn out a light when your brother is still peeing.

Do not play dodgeball with a baseball.

Do not try to jump over the backyard fence when you're jumping on the trampoline and someone double dog dares you to.

In fact, do not go through with any double dog dare. Being called a coward is better than being called dead.

Do not leap from the top bunk to the bottom one when the beds are perpendicular and the ceiling fan is on.

Do not try to ride a fan when it's turned on.

Do not ride your bike blindfolded.

I'm sure I've missed something. There are a million ways to die when you're a boy, but that's why I'm leaving you in the care of your daddy.

(On second thought, maybe I should brainstorm a bit longer.)

Dear Boys: I Love You Enough

Any time my boys feel angry at me for one reason or another (there are a billion of them), there's a familiar refrain that follows their rage: "You just don't love me."

When these words come racing from their mouth, their tongue tripping over syllables in their haste to make sure I know how very unloved they feel in this moment, I always have to work hard to stifle my laugh—because, on my best days, I'm a pretty empathic parent. On my worst, well, I feel like laughing at their ridiculous admissions and insights.

Sometimes I want to say, "Yeah, you're right. I don't love you. That's why I labored for thirteen hours with my eyeballs nearly popping out of my head so we could meet you before midnight. That's why I taught you to read, even though my teeth fell asleep while I tried to listen to you sound out a five-word sentence. That's why I carried you down the stairs when you asked every morning, even though my belly was being rearranged by twins and I couldn't see my feet. We could have both died, but you're right. I don't love you."

What I *really* want to do when they turn those hate-you eyes on me is list all the things that prove my love.

I love you enough to tell you that the crop top you have on actually belongs to your 3-years-younger brother.

I love you enough to listen to you use 15,000 words to tell me about a story you're writing that will probably only be 1,000 words long.

I love you enough to write a letter to you every year on your birthday.

I love you enough to insist on family pictures at least once a year so we can witness your growing up.

I love you enough not to buy that awkward school photo where you think you're smiling but it really just looks like you're mildly constipated.

I love you enough to keep all your elementary art projects tucked inside a bin in my closet.

I love you enough to laugh at all your made-up jokes.

I love you enough to let you wear two mismatching shoes just because you want to.

I love you enough to hide every pair of scissors in the house so you don't chop off a piece of your hair again and have to go to school looking like you're wearing a toupee you found in a cow pasture.

I love you enough to make you brush your teeth every night.

I love you enough to make sure you get enough sleep.

I love you enough to make you fold your own clothes and put them away yourself—because you'll never know how to do it until you try.

I love you enough to make you work out answers for yourself when you're stuck, instead of giving them to you right away.

I love you enough to snap that picture of you playing with the neighbor girl's Barbies—because gender lines don't matter.

I love you enough to forget about the time you said we should drop you off at an orphanage, because it would most likely be better than living in our house.

I love you enough to tell you that you should probably start wearing deodorant.

I love you enough to take your technology device away when you're not using it responsibly.

I love you enough to insist on a Play Outdoors time, a Silent Reading time, a Write in Journals time, and whatever else we come up with over the years.

I love you enough to tell you that washing under your arms and leaving the rest unwashed is not, in fact, a bath.

I love you enough to expose you to the vegetables you say taste like puke.

I love you enough to say, no, you may not wear your Spider-Man shirt for five days in a row.

I love you enough to let you know you'll probably regret not saving your money for that LEGO starship and, instead, spending it on a LEGO robot you didn't really want.

I love you enough to tell you stories and listen to yours until you finish (or very nearly).

I love you enough to put a hot home-cooked dinner in front of you every night, even though you'll likely complain about it before you've had a bite.

I love you enough to help you resolve conflicts with your brothers.

I love you enough to watch you make a fool of yourself in your Thanksgiving program at a religious preschool where Michael Jackson moves are not allowed.

I love you enough to bake a cake from scratch and then decorate it with a Mad Hatter's hat, even though it took three hours of my only day off and it was gone within the hour.

I love you enough to read all the books you tell me I should read, even if they have underpants and fart jokes and gross descriptions in them.

I love you enough to say yes.

I love you enough to say no.

I love you enough to say I'm sorry, enough, let's go, figure it out, it's okay to cry, it's not okay to scream, try it, you can do it, you can't do it, you can be whatever you want as long as you're willing to work hard at it, tell me about your day, what do you want, go outside, come in, I love you.

I love you.

And one day you'll know just how much.

What It Means to Be a Mom of Boys

I never thought I'd be a mom of all boys. When I first started my parenting journey, I thought for sure that I would have one or two girls in the mix, because everyone I know does. But then we had boy after boy after boy, and I realized, soon enough, that I was not meant to be a girl mom.

I was meant to be a boy mom. And there's something really special about boy moms.

1. You're the prettiest girl they've ever seen.

You'll always be the prettiest girl they've ever seen. You are the standard to which they will hold every other girl, at least for a while. They think you're beautiful when you've been wearing the same workout pants for three days in a row and when your hair hasn't been washed in a couple of days and when you don't even have makeup on. They think you're beautiful when you're in a bad mood and a silly mood and an I-don't-really-want-to-be-a-mother-today mood. They think you're beautiful because they see through a lens of love.

2. You will get grossed out daily.

Most kids are pretty gross, but boys are the worst. They don't care about the snot running all the way down to their chin; they'll just reach their little tongues up to "wipe" it away. They don't care that if they hug you, they're going to get a big slimy glob on your shoulder. They don't care that when they poop, they probably need at least three good wipes. They'll leave it at one and then stripe the toilet with the rest. Boys are pretty gross. Just get used to it.

3. You're a flower repository.

Every time you pass a wildflower field, boys will want to go pick as many flowers as they can and bring them back to you. They will want you to try to put those centimeter-long stems in your hair, even though they're too short to wrap around your ear. They will want you to put the pink ones in a vase so they can show off the bouquet to whomever may come to visit today, which is usually no one, because when you're a mom of boys, you're not often entertaining anyone else. Or maybe that's just me. Maybe I'm the only one afraid of social contact after being slimed all day by boys.

4. You will have regular exposure to potty humor or humor related to bodily functions.

Boys think all bodily humor is hilarious. And I mean all of it. If you make a farting sound between the lyrics to "Happy Birthday" while you're singing to their brother, they will fall apart giggling. If you end your prayers with an arm fart, or try to pretend like you're arm farting the ABC song, they will laugh until they're crying. If you say anything about "penis" or "naked booty," or "burp-farts," they will shriek with delight.

5. They're obsessed with their body parts. One in particular.

Not only do my boys love streaking through the house naked, even though they've been instructed to put on their pajamas directly after their bath so that we can get along to story time, they are fascinated by their body parts—well, one body part. They will play with their penises and compare penises and try to smack each other's penises just for the fun of it. They are uncivilized and untamable.

6. When you burp at the table, you feel like you've just won an award.

Boys will be contagiously delighted when their mom burps at the table. They think it's the funniest thing ever. Which is great, because holding in gas was never really my strong point. I always thought it was a flaw. Turns out it's not, because, that's right. Boys. I win the table every night, after the last bite. They'll laugh and applaud and I'll feel on top of the world, because I've never won anything in my life.

7. You get used to naked people.

As soon as the 6-year-old gets home from school, he likes to strip down to his boxers or underwear, whichever it is he's wearing for the day. He knows, of course, that he has to put on clothes to go outside, but that doesn't even matter. He'll choose a whole new ensemble if he goes outside, because those other clothes were the slightest bit damp from the walk home, and he "doesn't like to sweat."

The time just after baths in our house is a constant chorus of "Go put on your pajamas" and "Here are your pajamas. Put them on." and "You can't sit on my lap naked," because, well, boys just like the feeling of running free.

8. You don't get to hold them for long.

A few days after my youngest turned 1, he started coming over to give me a hug and then immediately squirming out of my arms before I was ready to let him go. Boys are active and rambunctious and prefer, always, to move. Every now and then I can entice this littlest one to stay a while, if I'm bouncing around or doing a ridiculous dance, or if I start running through the house, but if I'm not doing any of those things, he's not going to make an effort to stay.

Boys want to be moving at all times. I, on the other hand, don't. But I do want to snuggle with my boys every now and then, so sometimes I'll pick myself up off the floor, with great, sighing effort, and run around, too. Sometimes it's the only way I can steal a quick hug.

9. Disgusting smells become everyday smells.

My upstairs smells like a swamp, because there's a bathroom with a toilet up there that the boys always, always, always forget to flush. Their room smells like a locker room, because not only do they need to start wearing deodorant right about now, but they also like to wear their soccer socks for three days in a row, and, believe me, you haven't smelled disgusting until you've smelled worn-three-days-in-a-row soccer socks (or the shoes that have embraced them all day). Not only that, but whenever a boy is sitting on my lap, a cloud of fumes inevitably forms around us, because they're really, really good at SBDs (silent but deadlies—it's a type of fart you probably don't ever want to experience, in a class of its own). I can usually tell who's the culprit because of the self-satisfied smirk on his face while he looks around to see if anyone noticed. Of course we noticed. It smells like a sulfur plant in here. My nose hairs are singed.

Boys aren't easy. They're a whole lot of work. They require more energy than we'll probably ever have, because they never, ever stop. They're always getting into things, especially the food, and they're always making a mess, especially with the clothes they stripped off and left on the floor, and they're always asking us if we smelled that or if we want to see what they just did to the toilet (forever and ever answer: Nope.).

But the most amazing thing I've learned about boys is that they will love the insecurities right off a mama. They will love her doubts to disintegration. They will love away all that has come before and infuse hope into all that comes after.

I know, because that's what my boys have done for me.

And I'm so very glad.

The End

Don't miss out on a Crash Test Parents release! Visit www.crashtestparents.com to keep up-to-date on book and product releases and to access bonus material.

Appendix A: 13 Definitions that Will be Useful in Life With Boys

1. Tweapon (n.): A toy that becomes a weapon.
Ex: "Stop hitting your brother over the head with that tweapon," she said, grabbing Mr. Potato Head from her 4-year-old's hands.

2. Cryplaining (v.): Crying and complaining at the same time.
Ex: Every time we tell them what's for dinner, the boys start cryplaining.

3. Idiodare (v., n.): An idiotic dare.
Ex (v): I idiodare you to walk up the stairs in your roller blades.
Ex (n): The 9-year-old rode the skateboard down the stairs on an idiodare.

4. Silverwout (n.): Silverware that makes it outside but never seems to make it back inside.
Ex: How about we dig a hole in the backyard with the silverwout? Maybe with the fork-shovel.

5. Disopainience (n.): Doing something you've been told not to do and getting hurt in the process.
Ex: You hurt your finger when you stuck it in the box fan? That's the price of disopainience.

281

6. Twhining (v.): Talking while whining.
Ex: When the 4-year-olds miss their naps, they can't seem to say anything that doesn't sound like twhining.

7. Hungluttony (n.): When a kid asks for more and his plate is still full.
Ex: Before they've touched their first taco, my boys will ask for another. They have a bad case of hungluttony.

8. Fartinuous (n.): Continously fart. (v. Fartinuousing.)
Ex: Me to the boys: It's impressive that you can fartinuous, but I wish you would stop fartinuousing.

9. Laughiccup (v.): Laughing so hard you get the hiccups.
Ex: I can't help it. When my kid falls down, I laughiccup.

10. Candinapoopriate (adj.): When your kid says, very loudly while out in public, that he needs to go poop.
Ex: My 4-year-old's favorite place to be candinapoopriate is in the middle of a busy restaurant where everyone gets refried beans with their order.

11. Athletiformal (n.): Soccer socks, athletic shorts, button up shirt and a vest.
Ex: When my boys want to look "nice," they stick to athletiformal.

12. Themesumming (v.): Humming your own theme song.

Ex: When they're sitting on the toilet, my boys enjoy themesumming. You know, to encourage everything to come out alright.

13. Exmellyarmpits (n.): A spell that magically applies deodorant to a boy's underarms.

Ex: When my 9-year-old passes me smelling like a locker room and says he forgot to wear deodorant today, I exmellyarmpits him.

(I wish. He doesn't even remember to tell me he forgot.)

Appendix B: A Candid Question-and-Answer Session, Compiled from Real Conversations

Doctor: What are the ages of your kids?
Me: 9, 6, 5, 4-year-old twins, 14 months
Doctor: [jaw drop]
Me: Can I have my anxiety medicine now?

Person: Why do your kids look like orphans?
Me: We encourage free expression. Which means they get to dress themselves. Also, I'm too tired to care.

Person: What do you do with all that energy in your house?
Me: Wish it were mine.

Person: I bet your house is really loud.
Me: Well, I don't know. I just have to talk with a bullhorn. No big deal.

Person: Your house looks really great for having all these kids.
Me: You should have seen it ten minutes ago.

Person: What happened to your plants?
Me: That would be boys.

Person: Why are all the toilets in your house overflowing?
Me: Because my boys use an astronomical amount of toilet paper. Just ask Amazon Prime.

Person: You wanted a girl, didn't you?
Me: That's exactly why I had all these boys.

Person: How do you manage to get any work done?
Me: Duct tape. Works for everything.

Person: How do you handle all the talking?
Me: All at the same time.

Person [eyeing my six kids in a very obvious way]: Are you done?
Me: With what?

Person: When do you ever sleep?
Me: I'm a vampire. Just ask my kids.

Person: How do you feed them all?
Me: The only answer to that question is "All the time."

About the Author

Rachel is both the CBH (Chief Boy Herder) and CBP (Chief Boy Protector) in the Toalson home, simultaneously redirecting her boys from their quest to dig a backyard hole all the way to the earth's mantle—using the household forks—and attempting to convince them how unwise it is to follow through on their ideas without properly considering them first (in the last half-hour she has talked them out of doing a forward roll as their transport down the stairs, skating downhill with scooters—one for each foot—and trying to fly off the top of their treehouse with six pairs of underpants they duct-taped together). Her jobs are full-time jobs, which means she's in the market for a clone.

But when she's not trying to tame her tribe of wildlings, she writes essays, poetry, and fiction for both children and adults.

Rachel lives with her husband and six sons in San Antonio, Texas, where she writes at least 5,000 words a day, five days a week.

Author's Note

My dear reader,

I hope you have enjoyed this collection of stories about life with boys. I hope you have laughed out loud—laughed until you cried. I hope you have found a voice of solidarity threading through these pages—saying I see you, you are doing a great job, and you are not alone. I hope you have been encouraged, in some small way, by the precious gift of laugher. And I hope that from this day forward your laughter is endless, because in laughter—in humor—lives joy.

I write essays like the ones you've read in this book because parenting, most days, is hard. It often feels like there is no thanks, no reprieve, no victory to be had in the day after day, hour after hour of parenting young children. But laughter, I've found, is the best way to seize the moment, to embrace the struggle of raising decent human beings, and to find joy regardless of how many times we have to break up a slap-fight or tidy up the disastrous living room or listen to whining in the course of a day. Laughter turns the world toward joy.

Thank you for supporting my work. Please consider leaving a review wherever you bought it. Reviews help do a number of things—most notably get the book into the hands of other parents who might be struggling to live their daily reality with children in joy, in hope, and in love. Thank you for reading.

In love,
Rachel

Acknowledgments

While this book took hours of seclusion to write, rewrite, and rewrite again, it would not have been possible without:

My husband. You are a gracious and irreplaceable asset to my career, never telling me how crazy I am when I say, "I think I'm going to write another book."

My boys, who give me so much to laugh about I can scarcely write it down fast enough.

My mom, who nonchalantly said, "You should start writing all of that down like Erma Bombeck did."

My readers, who laugh right along with me.

I love you all madly.

Crash Test Parents

Enjoy more from the Crash Test Parents series:

www.crashtestparents.com

Are you a parent who needs a little dose of humor and hope?

For a limited time, pick up your FREE copies of *Guide to Surviving a Year* and *Guide to Self Esteem* and laugh your way back into hope. Or maybe just survival.

Get your FREE copies at:
racheltoalson.com/SurvivingAYear

www.ingramcontent.com/pod-product-compliance
Lightning Source LLC
Chambersburg PA
CBHW021430080526
44588CB00009B/481